IMAGES
of America

CLEVELAND NATIONAL FOREST

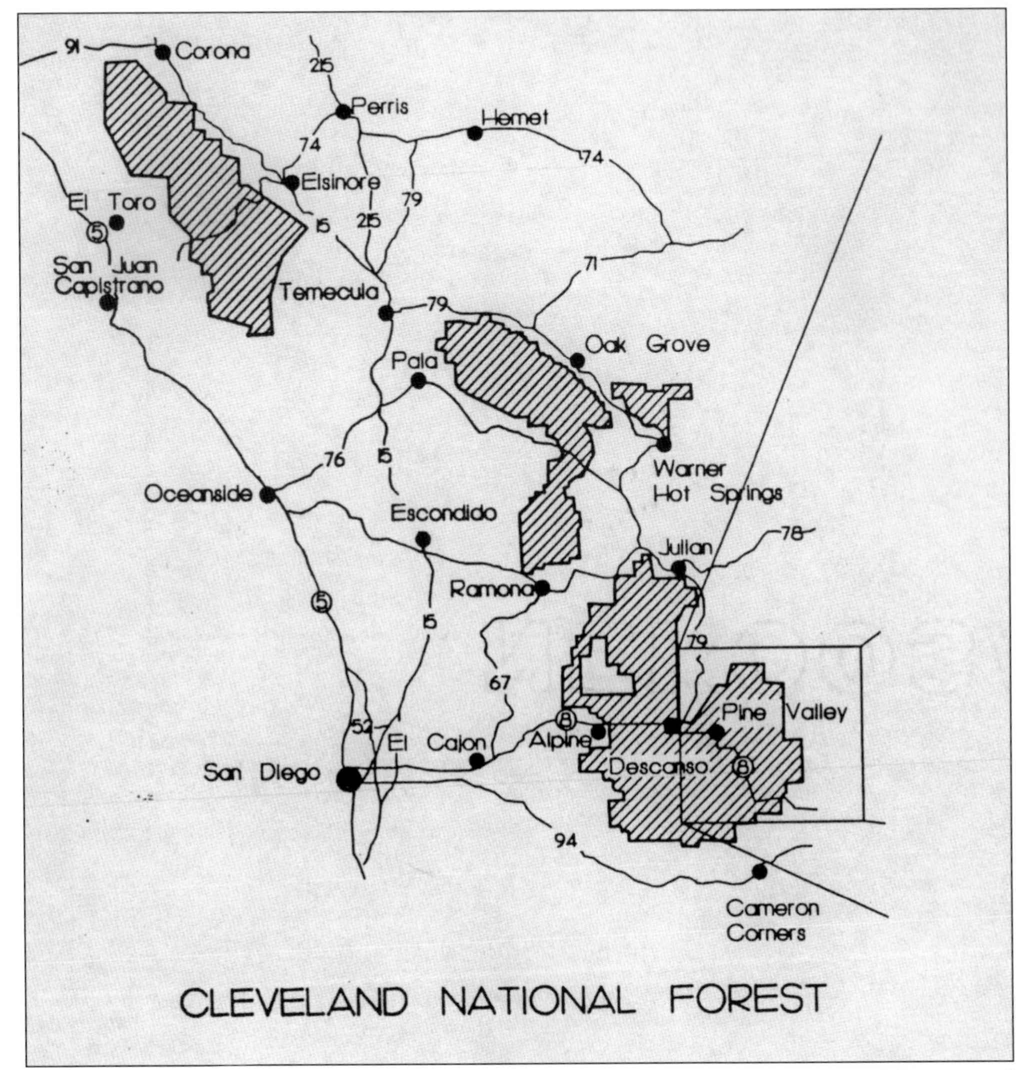

CLEVELAND NATIONAL FOREST MAP, C. 1995. From the Santa Ana Mountains of Orange and Riverside Counties at its northernmost reach, through the Palomar, Cuyamaca, and Laguna Mountains of central and eastern San Diego County, south to within 15 miles of the United States–Mexico border, the Cleveland National Forest (CNF) includes over 460,000 acres and stretches nearly 100 miles from top to bottom. (USDA-Forest Service.)

ON THE COVER: Forest superintendent Stephen Augustus "Gus" Nash-Boulden (fourth from right), along with his district rangers and permanent ranger staff, mounted up at the 1920 annual rangers meeting. Annual meetings provided an important opportunity to share information, provide training and management direction, and interact with the dispersed and isolated field staff during the early years. (USDA-Forest Service.)

IMAGES
of America

Cleveland National Forest

James D. Newland

ISBN 978-0-7385-5804-2

Published by Arcadia Publishing
Charleston SC, Chicago IL, Portsmouth NH, San Francisco CA

Printed in the United States of America

Library of Congress Catalog Card Number: 2007939178

For all general information contact Arcadia Publishing at:
Telephone 843-853-2070
Fax 843-853-0044
E-mail sales@arcadiapublishing.com
For customer service and orders:
Toll-Free 1-888-313-2665

Visit us on the Internet at www.arcadiapublishing.com

FOREST ENTRY AND BOUNDARY SIGN, C. 1960. Cut-stone masonry boundary signs were built using Civilian Conservation Corps (CCC) labor. These rustic-style stone signs are typical improvements from the 1930s onward. Although America was in the depths of the Great Depression, the Forest Service benefited from Pres. Franklin D. Roosevelt's New Deal conservation work program that provided much-needed jobs for young men from all over the country. During the nine years of its existence (1933–1942), the CCC employed over three million out-of-work young men in over 1,500 camps across the nation. The Departments of Agriculture and Interior, as well as state park agencies, were charged with overseeing the specific "work projects." For the USDA-Forest Service's 25-year-old Cleveland National Forest, this program, along with other Depression-era work-relief programs and funding, helped build a much-needed infrastructure, much of which still serves forest visitors and staff today.

Contents

ACKNOWLEDGMENTS

This book is the result of previous professional and volunteer work along with the support and assistance of many individuals, colleagues, and Forest Service professionals. First I must thank Margaret Hangan, former Cleveland Heritage Resources Program manager, for her enthusiasm, support, and reopening the forest's regionally significant archives and photographic collections for this project. Other Cleveland staff, including Anabele Cornejo, Susan Roder, and new forest supervisor Will Metz, have all provided access, knowledge, assistance, and encouragement. Regional historian Linda Lux has also been a vital supporter of me and this project. Historians, archivists, and friends who have provided assistance and inspiration from their previous and current efforts include Rich Borstadt, Mountain Empire Historical Society; Chris Travers, San Diego Historical Society; Dace Taube, University of Southern California Regional History Center; Bill Frank and Erin Chase, Huntington Library; Phil Brigandi, Orange County Archives; and historian/authors Jim Sleeper and John W. Robinson. Forest service historians Pam Connors and Dana Supernowicz, archaeologist/now district ranger Mike McIntyre of the Angeles National Forest, and archaeologist Bill Sapp of the San Bernardino National Forest—who made available the photographic archives of the Cleveland's sister forest—have all provided inspiration and support for me over the years and in this current undertaking. Thanks also go to those Cleveland managers, staff, and volunteers with whom I served in the mid-1990s. The creation of this book owes to the professional commitment and dedication shown me by former forest supervisor Anne Fege, Gary Vogt, Fred Coe, Lee DiGregorio, Mary Black, Judy Behrens, Gary Glotfelty, Joan Wynn, Susan Decker (see how important it was to catalog all those old photographs!), and the gentleman who instilled an appreciation for Forest Service history and its dedicated employees—Harvey Mack. But in large part, this book can be traced to former Heritage Program manager Cari VerPlanck—thanks for giving a young historian an opportunity. Finally, no greater thanks, and profession of love, can go to my wife, Jennifer, and daughter, Lindsay, for their sacrifices in letting me take the time for this book.

All photographs and graphics are from the archives of the USDA-FS Cleveland National Forest unless noted otherwise.

Foreword

It was once said, "Unless we practice conservation, those who come after us will have to pay the price of misery, degradation, and failure for the progress and prosperity of our day." And now nearly 100 years later, these words spoken by Gifford Pinchot, the first chief of the Forest Service, ring as true today as they did then. This idea of doing right by the land *today*, so that the land can thrive into the future, is crucial to protecting our forests in Southern California, across our nation, and truly around the world.

Challenges we face today are not terribly different than ones that our predecessors faced. Wildfires, driven by the Santa Ana winds, that burn thousands of acres seem commonplace to us living in greater Southern California. The question is not "if it burns," but rather "when it burns." However, you might be surprised that forestry reports from the 1870s through the 1890s also speak to large wildfires. These fires from more than 100 years ago ravaged water supplies and irrigation works, thus posing tough challenges to growing San Diego, Orange, and Riverside Counties. Sound familiar? Fire is a part of our natural ecosystem, just as tornados, hurricanes, and earthquakes. We must all learn to live with fire!

Our booming population is placing more demands on our limited natural resources. Just as Americans have always risen to a challenge, I am confident that today's Forest Service, partnered with the citizens of this tri-county region, will rise to meet these great conservation challenges of today, but will not stop there. I envision that we as one will go the extra mile to set new standards in land stewardship.

By order of Pres. Theodore Roosevelt, the Cleveland National Forest was established in 1908, and now, 100 years later, I am happy to report that the forest is alive and well. It is a biotic community that is thriving through its ability to adapt to the challenges before it. In the words of a wise conservationist, "a thing is right when it tends to preserve the integrity, stability and beauty of the biotic community. It is wrong when it tends otherwise." These words spoken by Aldo Leopold have been true in the past; they are true today; and they will continue to be true into the future. Let us not forget that we, too, as people, are a part of our biotic community. Join us as we celebrate the past 100 years of the Cleveland National Forest, and join us as partners as we move forward into the next 100 years.

—Will Metz, Forest Supervisor
Cleveland National Forest, 2008

RANGERS' VIEW, MOUNT PALOMAR, 1923. Southern California's timbered coastal and transverse mountain ranges drew American settlers as they had drawn the Native Americans and Hispanic pioneers before them. Views such as this fog-shrouded image of the peaks of the Palomar Mountains of San Diego County inspired the newest owners of the region to explore, occupy, and utilize the varied resources of these forested lands.

RANGER SCANNING THE ARID LANDSCAPE, C. 1910. Well-watered and timbered mountain valleys provided resources for early farmers, ranchers, and settlers in semi-arid Southern California. Starting in the 1880s, recreationists and health seekers also discovered the value of the open and wild forestlands of Orange, Riverside, and San Diego Counties. Such views of the arid desert lands reinvigorated the watershed protection mission of the Cleveland's early rangers.

Introduction

For over 100 years, the USDA-Forest Service's Cleveland National Forest has served as the administrative entity that manages the currently 460,000 acres of national forest lands in San Diego, Orange, and southwest Riverside Counties. For the millions of residents in the tri-county region embraced by the Cleveland National Forest, its existence, as well as its fundamental role in the urban development and environmental history of the region, is relatively unknown. This is the case, although hundreds of thousands of visitors make their way into the Cleveland each year to enjoy recreational facilities, scenic open space, and wilderness areas, or to revel at awe-inspiring and significant natural and cultural resources.

Yet, for many residents of the region, the Cleveland and the Forest Service only become relevant during the endemic, and often devastating, wildfire events that reintroduce the precarious relationship of urbanized Southern California to its native environment. As events such as the infamous 2003 Cedar fire and October 2007 firestorms have so tragically proven, the constant and inevitable growth of the region continues to expose the risks of living within Southern California's urban-wildland interface. How land management agencies such as the Cleveland National Forest work with each other, and the community at large, to reduce the vulnerability to such future conflagrations will be a continuing challenge as the second century of this story unfolds.

Not surprisingly, the urban-rural land management relationship is at the crux of the century-old story of the formation, development, and management of Southern California's national forests. As such, it is hoped that this centennial history of the Cleveland will not only serve as an ode to the dedicated men and women of the USDA-Forest Service, who have given so much to steward these invaluable public lands, but also provide a brief introduction and foundation for understanding the trials and tribulations that have evolved into the forest's management today. It may seem presumptuous, but it is the author's intention that this history also provide inspiration for those charged with tackling future forest management challenges—to remind us of the spirit, vigor, and dedication of those who have come before—and the challenges they overcame.

Historically, the Cleveland National Forest is a result of the growth of the conservation movement in the United States and the establishment and development of the national forest system. Active forest management in the United States dates to the mid-19th century. Scientists and scholars who studied the deforestation problems of Europe and the eastern United States wished to forgo a similar fate in the timber-rich western public domain. Feeding their concerns were abuses of the government's land distribution laws such as the Homestead Act of 1862 and the Timber and Stone Acts of the 1870s that opened millions of acres of public lands to private ownership for resource extraction, settlement, and development. Championing the concept of managing and conserving these resources for the public good, these "conservationists" lobbied national and state governments to set aside the nation's forest resources—conserving them for use by generations to come. In addition to the practical and scientific arguments, "aesthetic" conservationists such as writer George Perkins Marsh—whose influential 1864 book, *Man and Nature: The Earth as Modified*

By Human Action, heralded the perils of natural resource and wildland depletion— made strides in swaying public opinion toward the multiple values of conservation. The passage of the Forest Reserve Act of 1891, allowing the president to set aside federal forestlands as public reserves, was the culmination of a focused effort from conservationists, sportsmen, and forestry experts.

California served as a leader in the forestry and conservation movement during this period. Its scenic wonders and abundant forests and wildlands inspired many articulate and foresighted individuals to campaign for government protection of such resources and places. In 1864, Pres. Abraham Lincoln had been persuaded to grant the Yosemite Valley and Mariposa Grove of Big Trees to California as a state park. Still, as early as the 1870s, corporate accumulation of large tracts of public land, unrestricted grazing on the public domain, and the rapid proliferation of California's timber industry in response to the state's urban, industrial, and economic growth cautioned many Californians (mostly in the developing urban areas) to fear the permanent depletion of the state's forests. Over the next 40 years, men such as writer John Muir became prolific and eloquent voices in stirring public opinion for the forest and wildland conservation movement in California and the nation.

During this time, Southern California conservationists also played important roles in the support of these national and regional forest conservation efforts. Although depletion of the relatively small timber stands in the San Gabriel, San Bernardino, San Jacinto, Palomar, and Laguna Mountains were of concern, the major public outcry for conservation of Southern California's chaparral-covered "Elfin Forests" focused on protecting the local watersheds vital to the urban and agricultural development of the semi-arid region's coastal basins and valleys. Protection of the watershed led to widespread calls for prevention and suppression of wildland fires on unprotected public lands. Local leaders noted that such uncontrolled wildfires resulted in soil erosion, devastating post-fire floods, water table reduction, and loss of private property.

Lacking anti-forest lumber and mining interests that hampered forest reserve establishment in many Northern California forests, Southern California became a pioneering region in forest protection. Shortly after passage of the Forest Reserve Act, local forest and watershed protection proponents Abbot Kinney of San Gabriel and Theodore Lukens of Pasadena tapped regional support from civic and agricultural leaders to push for establishment of numerous forest reserves in Southern California. In 1892, Pres. Benjamin Harrison established the San Gabriel Forest Reserve, only the fourth created nationwide. Others followed, including the San Bernardino Forest Reserve in 1893 and Orange and Riverside County's Trabuco Canyon (1893) and San Jacinto (1897) Forest Reserves. It would be these last two pioneering forest reserves (the San Jacinto being extended into San Diego County in 1907) that on July 1, 1908, Pres. Theodore Roosevelt combined to form the Cleveland National Forest—named for pro-forest Pres. Grover Cleveland.

In the 100-plus years since its formation, the Cleveland has witnessed a diverse cast of protagonists ranging from the national stage, such as the aforementioned presidents, pioneer foresters such as Forest Service founder Gifford Pinchot, regional business and community leaders, and developers such as Abbot Kinney and John D. Spreckels, along with scores of local leaders, agencies, organizations, and individuals. But it has been the diverse and dedicated staff of Forest Service managers, rangers, technical experts, volunteers, and firefighters who have made the most indelible marks on the history of this land management institution and the surrounding communities.

This centennial history of the Cleveland National Forest makes use of the extensive forest archival photograph collection to provide but a brief visual introduction to the people, places, and events of this seminal public land management story.

One

The Fight for the Forest

Pre-1908

The history of the Cleveland National Forest's lands does not begin with its establishment in 1908. Archaeological and ethnographic studies indicate that local Native Americans had their own land management practices, including regular "light-burning" of brush. This changed with the arrival of Spanish Colonial settlers in 1769. Missionaries and soldiers introduced stock grazing and intensive agriculture practices along with a new social system that rapidly displaced native society, forever altering the centuries-old cultural landscape. After Mexican independence from Spain in 1821, new laws promoted private land holdings and foreign trade. Mexican Californios obtained rancho land grants that spread cattle ranching deeper into the backcountry. U.S. occupation of California in the late 1840s introduced a new set of cultural values, bringing more changes to the land, its resources, and its uses. American settlers took advantage of the Mediterranean climate to introduce marketable crops, develop the physical infrastructure to connect with the eastern United States, and thus increase the value of their lands. Starting in the 1850s, wagon roads east from San Diego and Los Angeles traversed around and through the future forest lands. Soon farmers, ranchers, and miners made their way into the mountains, setting up homesteads and forming small rural communities. In the 1880s, arrival of the transcontinental railroads triggered the first "Great Boom" of urban and agricultural development as waves of entrepreneurs, speculators, and developers descended on sparsely populated Southern California. This created a need to capture the irregular regional water resources, introducing concerns for protection of the forest watershed. As noted, local conservationists fought for, and obtained, protection for the forested lands in the 1890s, including the Trabuco Canyon and San Jacinto Forest Reserves. The establishment of these reserves, however, did not guarantee protection, with additional legislation required to authorize staffing the reserves. This political fight would be just the beginning for these early forest managers as they struggled not only to manage these reserves with minimal expertise and resources, but in fighting the unexpected opposition for bringing the forest reserve into San Diego County.

PIONEER CABIN, DOANE VALLEY, C. 1910S. Early settlers built homesteads and farms throughout the mountainous backcountry of 19th-century Southern California. Built by hand, these early homesteads provided shelter from the snowy winters and hot summers. This cabin, located in the valley named for self-proclaimed hermit-poet George Doane, provides an example of the rugged life of many of these pioneers.

"HOLY JIM" SMITH AND VISITORS, TRABUCO CANYON, C. 1900. The lands of the Cleveland feature stories and sites connected to many legendary characters. One of Orange County's notables from this time is "Holy Jim" Smith of Trabuco Canyon. Smith, on the far right, facetiously named for his hard life and use of "colorful language," established a homestead deep in Trabuco Canyon.

Keen Camp Schoolhouse, c. 1924. The one-room schoolhouse, such as this one at Keen Camp near Idyllwild in the San Jacintos, was a center of 19th-century rural community life. Schoolhouses often served as polling places, meeting halls, and community centers. Such schoolhouses could be, and still are, found throughout the rural communities within and around the Cleveland National Forest.

Campo Cowboys, c. 1890. Many early settlers made their livelihoods through cattle and sheep ranching. Pictured from left to right, Archie Chilwell, Archibald Campbell, and Manual Ortega were descendants of pioneering Campo cattle ranchers who had claims upon and grazed the public lands of the Laguna Mountains since the 1870s. Campbell and Chilwell would later establish the successful Campo Cattle Company. (Mountain Empire Historical Society.)

SAWMILL SITE, SAN JACINTO, C. 1910. Timber stands in the mountains of the tri-county region were small compared to Northern California. The largest stands of marketable timber could be found in the San Jacintos, the site of this early sawmill operation. The smaller timber stands in the Palomar and Laguna Mountains were rapidly tapped, triggering fears from locals that these areas would be deforested by the 1880s.

CITRUS GROVES BELOW THE SANTA ANAS, 1921. By the 1880s, Southern California's agricultural interests, especially the profitable citrus industry, were a major economic force—fueling the region's demographic and urban development. Civic and agricultural leaders banded together with conservationists who wished to protect the forest and brush lands from destructive land use practices to maximize limited water resources.

Wildfire Viewed from Point Loma, 1910. Euro-American explorers of the 18th century first documented Southern California wildfires. Starting in the 1870s, newspapers reported on the numerous, apparently annual, and destructive brush fires that burned uncontrolled for days and weeks, destroying homesteads and ranch lands. Such events prompted calls from both rural and urban residents for government assistance with fire control and prevention.

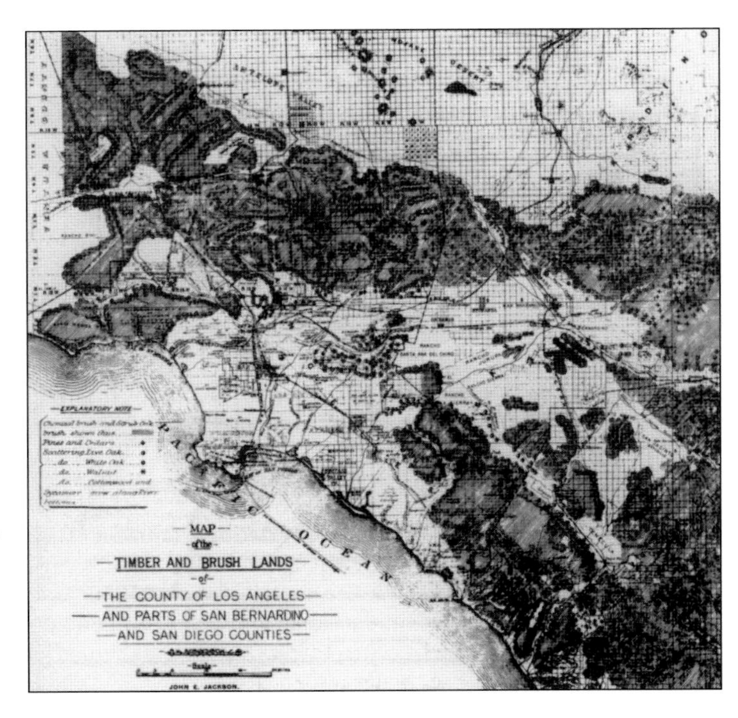

Southern California Timber and Brush Lands Map, 1886. Concerns about unbridled consumption of timber, overgrazing, and the need for wildfire control on California's large public domain stirred conservationists statewide. In 1885, Gov. George Stoneman formed the California State Board of Forestry to help manage the state's forests. The early years of the board focused its efforts on documenting forest resources.

ABBOT KINNEY, STATE FORESTRY BOARD COMMISSIONER. In May 1886, Stoneman appointed staunch forest and watershed proponent Abbot Kinney of San Gabriel to the board. Kinney was a citrus farmer, botanist, and land developer. A world traveler and adventurer, he is usually remembered for accompanying author/activist Helen Hunt Jackson on her travels through Southern California—and for his development of the Southern California beach community of Venice. Kinney focused the board on the effects of deforestation on water supply. After Kinney was removed from the board for political reasons in 1890, he campaigned for federal forest protection for Southern California. Federal forestry had gained standing when the Department of Agriculture established the Division of Forestry in 1881. In 1886, Bernard Fernow, the first professional forester in the division, was named chief. Fernow was instrumental in working with the Department of the Interior's General Land Office to obtain legislation (the Forest Reserve Act of 1891) to set aside and protect the nation's forest reserves. (Henry E. Huntington Library.)

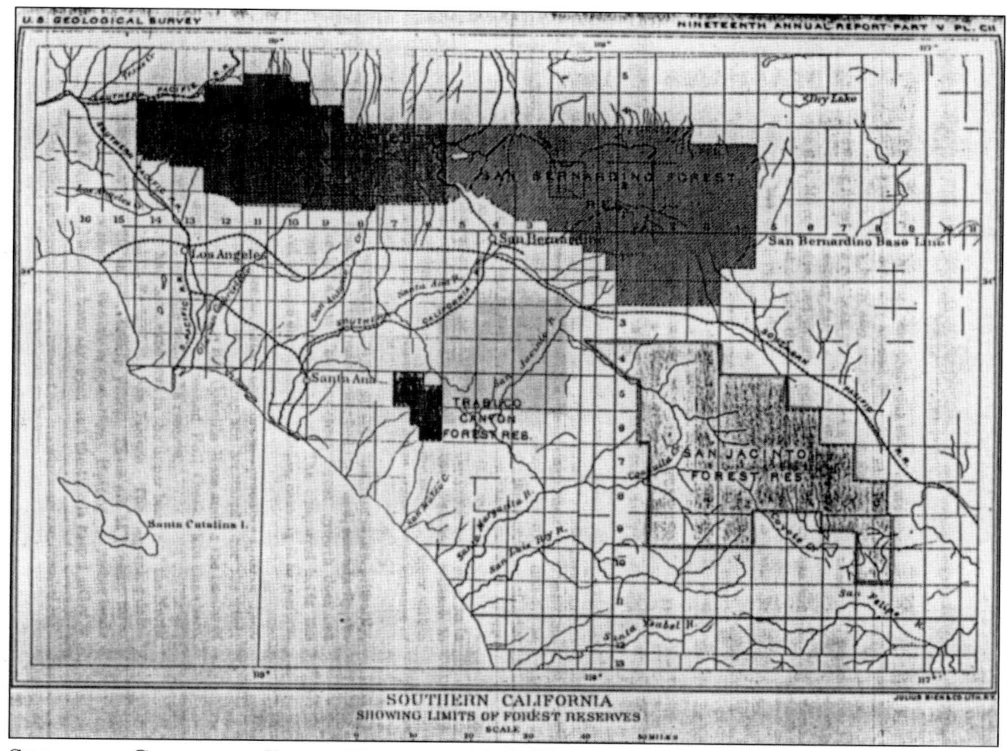

SOUTHERN CALIFORNIA FOREST RESERVES, 1898. With the Forest Reserve Act in place, Kinney lobbied for federal forest reserves to protect Southern California's irrigation and water supply. The General Land Office responded, sending Iowa banker and land law expert Benjamin F. Allen. Allen's initial survey reports resulted in President Harrison creating the San Gabriel, San Bernardino, and the future Cleveland's Trabuco Canyon Reserves.

PRES. GROVER CLEVELAND, C. 1890S. The Forest Reserve Act allowed the president to "reserve" any forest-bearing public lands. Pres. Benjamin Harrison used the act to create 15 reserves totaling over 13 million acres by spring 1893. His successor, Grover Cleveland, earned his place in forest history with his proclamation of 13 new "Washington's Birthday" forest reserves on February 22, 1897.

Benjamin F. Allen, 1903. The Forest Reserve Act did not authorize staffing the reserves. In June 1897, President McKinley signed the bill confirming Cleveland's reserves, including the 737,280-acre San Jacinto Forest Reserve—although locals had not actively pursued this reserve. This Forest Management Act authorized reserve staffing. Allen was quickly named special agent for California's and the Southwest's reserves. (*Los Angeles Times*, November 14, 1903.)

First Supervisor Grant Taggart and Ranger, 1898. Allen arrived in Los Angeles in June 1897. In summer 1898, the General Land Office authorized him to hire the first forest supervisors and rangers. Grant I. Taggart (left) was the first supervisor for the San Jacinto and Trabuco Canyon Reserves. Here he and one of his rangers inspect the San Jacintos. (Henry E. Huntington Library.)

TAGGART WITH RANGER "CON" SILVAS, 1898. Typical of early reserve supervisors, Taggart was a political appointee—from Northern California. The ranger staff, however, was generally chosen from local men. One of the first San Jacinto hires was Charles H. Thomas Jr., son of local pioneers. Ranger Jose Maria "Con" Silvas was a Soboba Indian familiar with the San Jacinto backcountry. (Henry E. Huntington Library.)

EARLY "VAQUERO" RANGERS, 1905. Early rangers focused on wildfire prevention and controlling illegal grazing and burning. They received little management direction from General Land Office administrators and relied on skills typically associated with cowboys. They were paid $50 per month but were required to provide their own horse, gear, and supplies and spent much time in the saddle, camping out in the reserve.

Forest Rangers, Trabuco Reserve, c. 1904. The 49,479-acre Trabuco Canyon Reserve was one of the earliest, yet smallest, reserves, barely covering the Santa Ana Mountain peaks. Rangers from the San Jacinto patrolled the smaller reserve. In January 1899, President McKinley nearly doubled the acreage to further protect the lands in response to complaints of burning and overgrazing by local "sheepmen."

Early Ranger Station, Tahquitz Valley, 1903. This old cattlemen's cabin in Tahquitz Valley served as a "ranger station" during the initial years. The General Land Office (GLO) formed its "Division R" to oversee reserve management. However, with little early funding and planning direction, few provisions were made for establishing formal ranger stations, forcing rangers to be creative and opportunistic.

SAN DIEGO CHAMBER OF COMMERCE RESOLUTION, 1901. Local civic and business leaders led the drive for a forest reserve in the Palomar and Laguna Mountains. These prominent men saw the value of the mountain watershed to their regional development plans. This chamber resolution supports Supervisor Taggart's initial reports recommending extension of the San Jacinto Reserve into San Diego County.

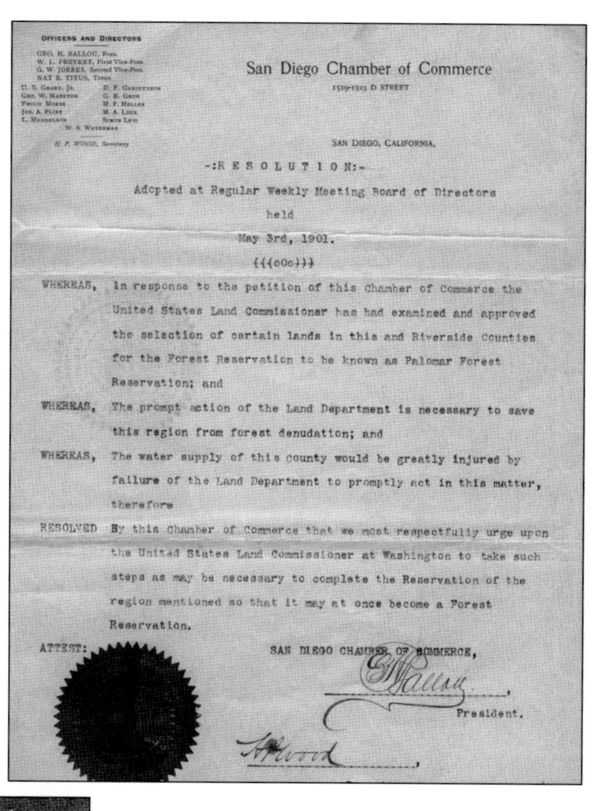

OFFICERS AND DIRECTORS

GEO. H. BALLOU, Pres.
W. L. FREVERT, First Vice-Pres.
G. W. JORRES, Second Vice-Pres.
NAT R. TITUS, Treas.

U. S. GRANT, Jr. | D. F. GARRETTSON
GEO. W. MARSTON | G. B. GROW
PHILIP MORSE | M. F. HELLER
JOS. A. FLINT | M. A. LUCE
L. MENDELSON | SIMON LEVI
W. S. WATERMAN

H. P. WOOD, Secretary

San Diego Chamber of Commerce

1519-1523 D STREET

SAN DIEGO, CALIFORNIA,

-:R E S O L U T I O N:-

Adopted at Regular Weekly Meeting Board of Directors
held
May 3rd, 1901.
{{{oOo}}}

WHEREAS, In response to the petition of this Chamber of Commerce the United States Land Commissioner has had examined and approved the selection of certain lands in this and Riverside Counties for the Forest Reservation to be known as Palomar Forest Reservation; and

WHEREAS, The prompt action of the Land Department is necessary to save this region from forest denudation; and

WHEREAS, The water supply of this county would be greatly injured by failure of the Land Department to promptly act in this matter, therefore

RESOLVED By this Chamber of Commerce that we most respectfully urge upon the United States Land Commissioner at Washington to take such steps as may be necessary to complete the Reservation of the region mentioned so that it may at once become a Forest Reservation.

ATTEST: SAN DIEGO CHAMBER OF COMMERCE,

G H Ballou, President.

H P Wood,

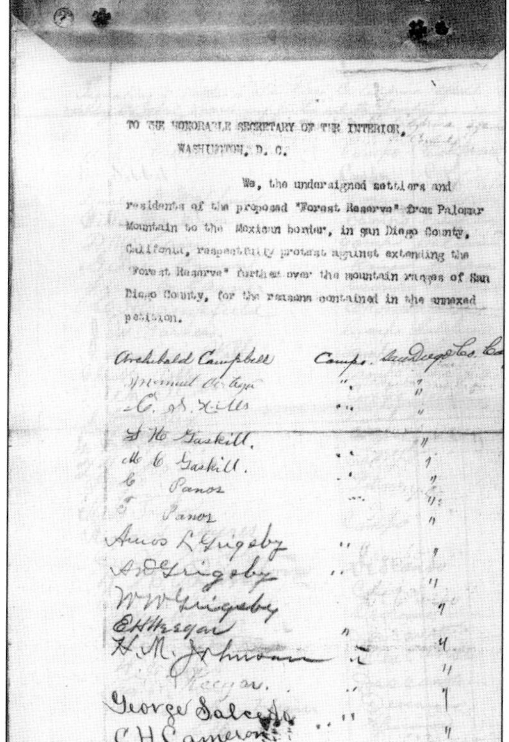

TO THE HONORABLE SECRETARY OF THE INTERIOR,
WASHINGTON, D. C.

We, the undersigned settlers and residents of the proposed "Forest Reserve" from Palomar Mountain to the Mexican border, in San Diego County, California, respectfully protest against extending the "Forest Reserve" further over the mountain ranges of San Diego County, for the reasons contained in the annexed petition.

Archibald Campbell Campo. San Diego Co. Ca

ANTI-FOREST PETITION, 1901. The forest reserve extension did not receive unanimous support. In September 1901, Campo and Laguna Mountain rancher Archibald Campbell became the spokesman for backcountry ranchers against the reserve. Pioneer ranchers from Campo, Descanso, Julian, and Mesa Grande signed the petitions that garnered support from local senators and congressmen to direct GLO commissioner Binger Herrmann to reject the proposal that October.

GIFFORD PINCHOT, C. 1900. In 1903, the Bureau of Forestry sent Inspector Ralph Hosmer to reevaluate the San Diego County forests. Prominent pro-forest citizens such as J. D. Dodson, F. W. Scripps, George Marston, and M. A. Luce rallied support, including a well-publicized September visit from bureau chief Gifford Pinchot. Pinchot's inspirational speech eased fears and reinvigorated the study for reserve extension south to the Mexican border.

PRESIDENT ROOSEVELT WITH PINCHOT, C. 1905. As early as 1901, Pinchot's powerful friends openly supported his plan to transfer the forest reserves to the Department of Agriculture. On February 1, 1905, President Roosevelt approved the transfer, creating the USDA's U.S. Forest Service. In 1907, all reserves were renamed national forests, emphasizing Pinchot's philosophy of conservation for use—not "reserving" the public from their lands.

TRABUCO CANYON NATIONAL FOREST MAP, 1907. In 1906, Forest Service agent Robert Ayers reported on the smaller Trabuco Reserve. He noted only one permanent ranger assigned, leading to Orange County residents' frustrations over lack of patrol and fire control. Ayers recommended a 45,000-acre addition and dedicated staffing for the isolated east and west ranges. On July 14, 1907, President Roosevelt approved the extension.

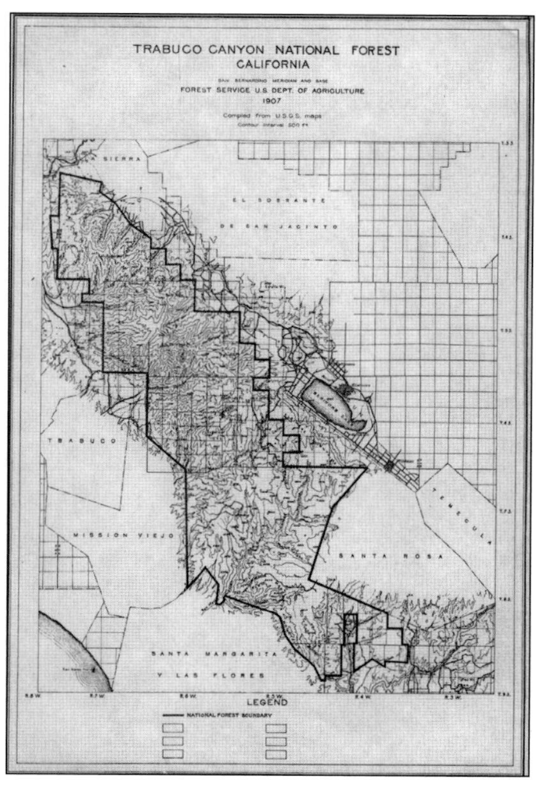

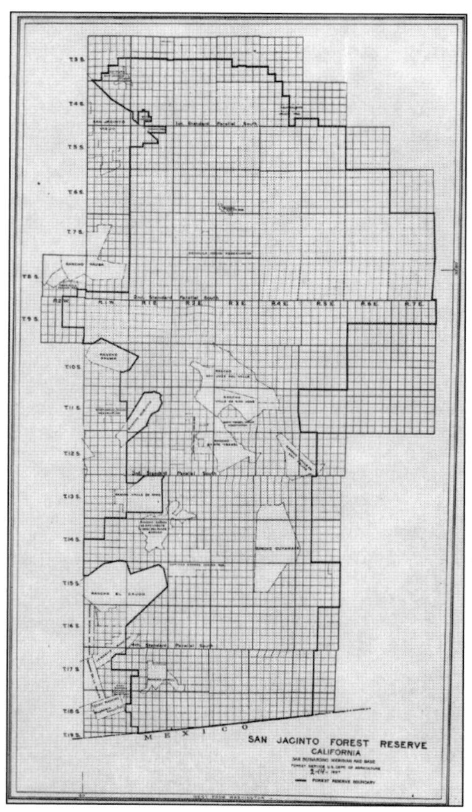

ENLARGED SAN JACINTO NATIONAL FOREST, 1907. Pinchot's 1903 visit triggered extensive studies of San Diego's forest and watershed. Citing expected regional growth, forestry and GLO officials recommended a 1.1-million-acre extension. On February 14, 1907, President Roosevelt signed the proclamation adding nearly all of San Diego County's federal land east of Escondido and El Cajon to the San Jacinto National Forest.

CLEVELAND NATIONAL FOREST RANGER MEETING, 1910. Regular meetings with the isolated forest staff became key for early managers. Pinchot also created a "Use Book" for rangers outlining the mission, goals, and practices of the Forest Service while attempting to place trained foresters into supervisor positions. In October 1907, Pinchot named India-born British immigrant Harold A. E. Marshall as superintendent of the San Jacinto and Trabuco Canyon National Forests.

(COPY)

UNITED STATES DEPARTMENT OF AGRICULTURE
FOREST SERVICE
CLEVELAND NATIONAL FOREST

San Diego, Cal.,

July 1, 1908

To all Forest officers,

Cleveland National Forest.

Dear Sir:

By order of the Forester, effective July 1, 1908, the San Jacinto and Trabuco Canyon National Forests will be consolidated under one name, and will hereafter be known as the Cleveland National Forest.

Please make this known as widely as possible, and if possible, request the newspaper in your locality to publish it as a news item, bing sure that no charge will be made for such insertion.

Very respectfully,

/s/ HAROLD A. E. MARSHALL

Forest Supervisor.

CLEVELAND NATIONAL FOREST RENAMING ORDER, JULY 1, 1908. From 1905 to 1908, national forest acreage tripled nationally. In an effort to manage the enormous, decentralized Forest Service administration, Pinchot worked with Roosevelt to combine numerous national forests. After pro-forest Pres. Grover Cleveland passed away on June 24, 1908, Roosevelt signed a proclamation renaming the combined Trabuco Canyon and San Jacinto National Forest for him.

Two

EARLY YEARS OF THE CLEVELAND 1908–1932

The "Cleveland" was up and running, although locals in Orange County and the San Jacintos protested the loss of their individual geographic national forest monikers. In January 1909, forest supervisor Marshall sent a status report on the six-month-old Cleveland National Forest to the district (regional) forester in San Francisco. Marshall noted the resources and goals of the newly combined national forest. The Cleveland's lands were the main supplier of water to over 60,000 residents of three Southern California counties. The imminent completion of the Panama Canal and the San Diego and Arizona Railroad directly east from San Diego to the Imperial Valley was expected to expand the local populations exponentially, making the region's water resources even more valuable. Within the then over two million acres of Cleveland National Forest lands were small but valuable timber stands in the San Jacinto, Palomar, Cuyamaca, and Laguna Mountains. Fire and overgrazing claimed Marshall's main focus, although managing agricultural, ranching, and mining interests also required attention. Marshall commented that the growing mountain resort industry and easier access to the formerly remote forest through the automobile would likely make recreation a growing management concern. Marshall's analysis of the land use management requirements of the Cleveland have changed little over the years and provided the direction for the establishment of today's forest administration. It was during these 25 years that Marshall, his successors, and their staffs created—often through extensive trial and error, experience and study, and planning and implementation—the foundations on which the forest was built. It is these stories of the pioneering men and women of this period that detail the struggles with defining the forest boundaries, creating manageable administrative districts, developing a previously nonexistent infrastructure for transport, communication, fire control, and recreation, setting and enforcing forest rules and regulations, and all the while helping to build public support for the mission and goals of the fledgling institution with minimal staff and funding—all traditions that, for better or worse, have remained hallmarks of managing the Cleveland National Forest.

CNF PERMANENT STAFF, 1910. This staff portrait from the 1910 annual meeting illustrates the hearty forest rangers of the early years. Present were forest pioneers such as Rangers J. R. Bell, John Maxfield, A. W. Bartlett, and Con Silvas. They were joined by "new" men who would spend many years earning legendary status for service on the Cleveland, such as Supervisor Harold Marshall and Rangers J. B. Stephenson, Carl Brenner, Ed Miller, and Ben Johnson.

SUPERVISOR MARSHALL LEADING INSPECTION RIDE, 1910. Marshall's first task was to establish an administrative system for managing over two million acres within three counties. Early supervisors and rangers usually lived in towns closest to their forests and patrol "districts." Rangers tried to identify sites with known water and available feed for potential administrative use.

FOREST SERVICE SURVEYORS IN MASON VALLEY, C. 1910. Confirming forest boundaries and classifying its lands were a primary task. The 1907 expansion into San Diego County simply placed all government land east of Escondido and El Cajon within the forest. Here surveyors confirm the arid nature of the lands east of the Laguna Mountains—land later included in Anza-Borrego Desert State Park.

SAN JACINTO RANGERS SURVEYING HOMESTEAD CLAIM, 1911. The Forest Homestead Act of June 11, 1906, was responsible for much early classification work. Sponsored by anti-forest interests, it allowed individuals to acquire up to 160 acres of national forest land if classified as "agricultural." Many individuals took advantage of this law to establish homesteads, farms, and ranches during the few years this law was active.

FEDERAL MEN SURVEYING MEXICAN BORDER NEAR CAMPO, 1910. The Cleveland's original boundaries extended to the U.S. border with Mexico. This photograph shows cooperative work between the Forest Service, Customs Service, and Bureau of Animal Industry (BAI) in surveying the border, building fence, and setting monuments. The BAI was responsible for health inspections of imported stock.

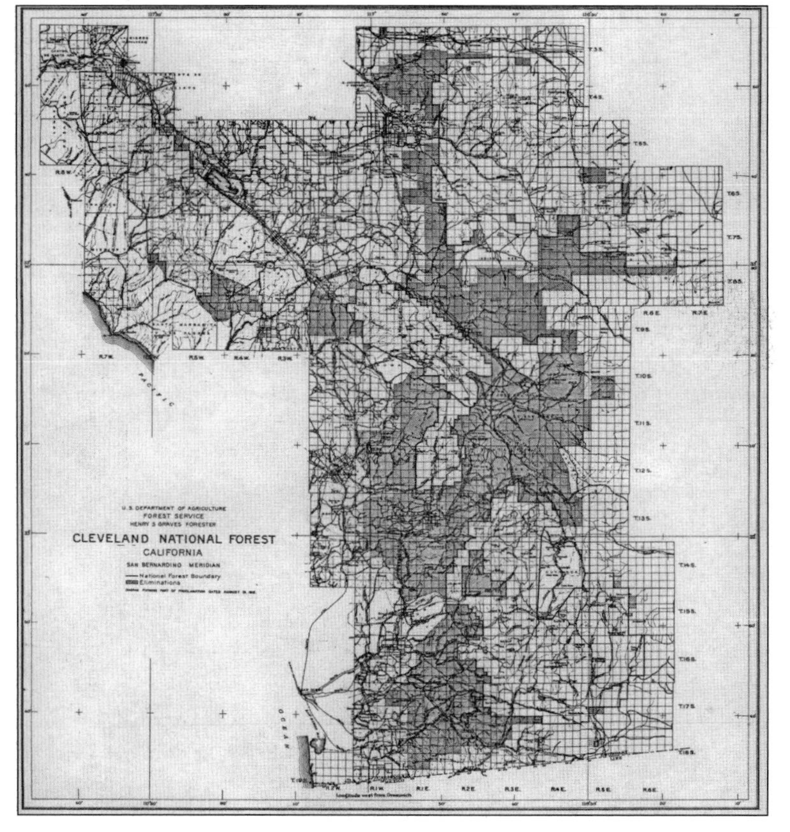

FOREST ELIMINATION MAP, 1915. From 1909 to 1919, the Cleveland Forest boundaries were altered through seven separate presidential proclamations or executive orders, the largest being the 1912 elimination removing the desert lands east of the Lagunas and San Jacinto Mountains and the border areas around Dulzura and Campo. The August 31, 1915, eliminations are shaded on this map.

EARLY SAN JACINTO NATIONAL FOREST STATION, C. 1910. The early Supervisor's Office had a vagabond existence. The San Jacinto National Forest office moved between Hemet, San Jacinto, and Valle Vista. In mid-1908, Supervisor Marshall relocated the Supervisor's Office to San Diego, moving into the new Federal Building downtown in 1913. Supervisor W. H. Sloane moved the office to Escondido in 1915. It returned to San Diego in 1919.

BANNING RANGER STATION, C. 1910. Prior to 1917, the Forest Service did not have standard plans for administrative buildings or sites. With horses, mules, and field stock needed for transportation, packing, and farming, early stations resembled homesteads. This photograph shows the station house, barn, windmill, and hay field. This well-suited administrative site was leased from the Bureau of Indian Affairs.

KEEN CAMP RANGER STATION, WINTER 1910. Keen Camp was the first permanent station in the district, completed in 1907–1908. This site, just south of Idyllwild, provided access to the Mount San Jacinto region. The station included a typical American "hall and parlor"–style residence/station building along with a barn, storage, and outbuildings.

SAN JACINTO RANGER STATION, 1922. San Jacinto served as the district office from 1908 until the construction of Idyllwild Station in 1934. It was one of the first stations in the forest to be built under the 1917 guidelines for "standard plan" buildings that regional forester Coert DuBois had established for improving California's Forest Service facilities.

LAS LOMAS MUERTAS STATION, 1911. Located near the foot of Bottle Peak on the western edge of the Palomar Mountains, the Las Lomas Muertas Station was typical of many early administrative sites. This photograph shows a seasonal tent cabin that served as both residence and district office. Ranger George Park poses with his mount in front of the recently opened station.

LAS LOMAS MUERTAS STATION BARN, 1911. Illustrating early facility priorities, this "permanent" wooden barn was constructed along with the Tent House. In 1912–1913, Ranger Park worked to build a permanent residence building. Unfortunately, as also typical, the station was abandoned after the 1915 eliminations placed it far from the forest boundary.

OAK GROVE RANGER STATION, c. 1925. The nearly 40-acre Oak Grove Administrative Site was withdrawn in 1906. In 1908, rangers built the first residence, barn, and a tree nursery and plantation. Located along the old Southern Immigrant Stage Road (now State Route 79), it served as the Palomar District Office from 1915 to 1950.

POST OFFICE CANYON HAY FIELD, c. 1920. Not all administrative sites served as ranger stations. Some sites were needed to provide feed for the large numbers of required stock. This hay field served this early-day necessity. Such farming duties were requirements of early rangers in addition to firefighting, range management, surveying, improvement work, and general patrol.

EL TORO RANGER OFFICE, C. 1920. The rugged Santa Ana Mountains provided the Trabuco District administrative challenges. Until Ortega Highway opened in 1933, the district was managed in west and east ranges. Ranger J. B. Stephenson and son William pose in front of the home Stephenson built on his own lot that served as the west side office until his transfer in 1922.

CORONA STATION, 1925. Eastside rangers usually rented homes in Corona or Elsinore, using remote La Cienega and El Cariso stations seasonally. Corona was identified as a possible district office site in 1909. The forest purchased a lot in 1921, and this station house and garage were completed in 1925. From then until 1960, and again after 1983, Corona served as the Trabuco District Office.

Campo Ranger Station, c. 1910. The 1907 expansion added the future Descanso District lands. Early administrative sites included border communities such as Dulzura, Tecate, Potrero, and Campo. By 1910, new "standard" residences such as this one, believed to be located at Campo, were also completed at Dulzura and Chiquito (Descanso). The 1912 eliminations forced the sale of the Dulzura and Campo stations.

Interior, Chiquito Residence, 1910. This rare interior photograph of the Chiquito (Descanso) residence is a glimpse into the private lives of early rangers. The mantle loaded with family photographs, the stone rubble–faced fireplace, rocking chairs, panel drapes, lace doilies, and metal-frame bed set a scene of domestic bliss. Such facilities were rare and generally reserved for district rangers.

RANGER BRENNER AND FAMILY, C. 1910. In 1912, Inspector L. A. Barrett wrote of Carl Brenner's financial challenges as typical of early ranger sacrifices. Brenner earned $1,100 annually with living expenses of $990. As such, he kept a cow and chickens, shoed his own horses, and made the most of his $75 allotment for horse and livestock expenses to stretch his $110 of "spending money."

DESCANSO STATION, 1920S. In 1915, Descanso became the district office. With the advent of the automobile, the Descanso Station was perfectly located along the main east-west transportation route (State Highway 12, then U.S. 80 starting in 1926). The district office remained here until the opening of Interstate 8, when it was moved to Alpine.

EL PRADO CABIN, 1920s. The Laguna Mountains was the other area to receive special planning and facility development. In 1909, forest administrators withdrew 80 acres in the Laguna Meadow. In 1911, rangers constructed this simple log cabin at El Prado Meadow for seasonal use. It served as the main station in the Lagunas until the 1920s.

RANGER MILLER'S BEST FRIEND, c. 1915. Ranger work often required traveling alone in remote locations. As such, canine companions were helpful in many ways for tracking animals, locating lost visitors, and "rooting out" snakes. Many rangers kept dogs as part of their "staff." Here Ranger Ed Miller enjoys a lighter moment with his trusty friend.

Ranger Ben Johnson and His Four-Legged Partner, 1914. Ranger Ben Johnson poses proudly with his horse. Early rangers were required to spend significant time in the saddle. A good horse was an essential partner for a ranger's success. Prior to development of truck trails, rangers accomplished almost all their work from horseback.

Packing Materials for Lookout, c. 1910s. Without roads and automobiles, all supplies, materials, and equipment for remote facilities such as fire lookouts were packed in via horse and mule. Lumber and equipment were negotiated on pack mules for this early lookout located above Warner's Hot Springs on the Palomar District.

Hauling Telephone Poles, c. 1920. Communication was key for fire detection and firefighting. Rangers, including J. B. Stephenson here, were trained in building and repairing simple telephone systems used to connect stations to fire lookouts. Expanding and maintaining such a system was essential as rangers would access the lines using portable phones that could be spliced in at any pole or tree.

Uncooperative Mule, Santiago Peak Trail, c. 1920. This photograph indicates that stereotypes sometimes have real inspiration. The note on the back of this photograph simply states "stubborn mule." This ranger works to coerce this "reclining" pack mule to continue on his trip to Santiago Peak to deliver supplies to the lookout.

EARLY OFF-ROADING, C. 1920. Entering the 1920s, the automobile became a new tool for forest managers. Here rangers test out a solid-tire coupe on a rough fire trail in heavy chaparral. Staff soon looked to heavy trucks and autos that could traverse the rough roads and be fitted to meet their specific needs in road building, inspection, and fire control.

GRAZING AND EROSION, C. 1930. Cleveland Forest managers' watershed protection mission made erosion control a prime concern. For the brush-covered mountains of Southern California, lack of vegetation equaled severe erosion from infrequent but powerful winter storms. This placed ranchers at odds with foresters who connected overgrazing and burning-off brush for grass and feed with watershed destruction.

CROUCH MEADOW "EROSION PLUG," 1923. Erosion control was a focus for all forest uses. Rangers were trained in erosion control basics. Check-dams were implemented to reduce soil erosion and protect water tables. Forest policies were controversial for not only range users but for locals who feared large fires. Such policies led local critics to derogatorily refer to Cleveland rangers as "brush herders."

RANGE ASSESSMENT WORK, DYCHE VALLEY, C. 1910S. Range management proved contentious for early Cleveland managers. Here a ranger assesses the condition of forest rangeland. Rangers experienced animosity from the well-entrenched stockmen of eastern San Diego County. Many of the same ranchers who had fought the establishment of the forest continued their opposition to federal permitting and grazing rules into the 1920s.

BRUSH FIRE THREATENING RAMONA, 1913. Southern California fires were well documented since the 1870s, but not until the disastrous fire season of 1910 (which burned nearly five million acres, killed hundreds, and destroyed significant private property nationally) would the Forest Service develop formal fire management practices. With the Cleveland's fire vulnerability, the forest staff became early implementers and innovators in fire control.

RANGER POSTING FIRE WARNING, C. 1910. Forest Service officials began studying effects and methods of fire management in the 1910s. California fire control pioneers, such as regional forester Coert DuBois and assistants Stuart B. Show and Roy Headley, were instrumental in implementing cutting-edge fire control systems featuring fixed-point lookouts, fire trails and breaks, crew tactics, field communication, regulation enforcement, and public education.

BOUNDARY SIGNS WITH FIRE WARNINGS, C. 1910S. The Forest Service's mission and goals were generally unknown. In order to help visitors understand and enforce forest rules, regulations, and policies, forest managers posted signs such as these. In addition, a cooperative relationship with the Automobile Club of Southern California helped erect signs that were both informational and supported management practices.

CUTTING FIRE BREAK, C. 1928. Fire prevention and suppression became the major forest activity. Fire control directed most forest improvement work, such as laying telephone lines, cutting fire breaks and trails, and locating and building lookouts. Prior to the advent of trucks and tractors in the late 1920s, all of this work was accomplished using hand-crew labor.

FIRE CREW, TRABUCO DISTRICT, C. 1920. Most fire crews were made of local men recruited and trained by permanent staff. The establishment of the California Department of Forestry in 1905 and local fire prevention ordnances and departments in the tri-county areas during these early years helped initiate cooperative fire control relationships to support Forest Service fire suppression and prevention activities.

NATURE'S FIRE LOOKOUT, 1910. Forest fire management plans included establishing fixed-point fire lookouts atop strategic mountain peaks or high points. This photograph in the Descanso District illustrates the creativity of early rangers lacking facilities and budgets. Lookouts provided early detection of fires, allowing quicker responses to reduce fire acreage, improve protection of property, and direct strategic suppression efforts.

Hot Springs Fire Lookout, 1913. Hot Springs Lookout above Warner's Hot Springs was the first lookout structure on the Cleveland. Ranger Edward Bish designed and constructed the roughly eight-by-eight-foot lookout cab in 1912. He, and other lookouts, lived in a tent near the cab for the six-month fire season.

Lyons Peak Lookout, 1913. Additional lookouts followed at Santiago Peak on the Trabuco District, Bottle Peak near Palomar Mountain, and here at Lyons Peak on the Descanso. This five-by-five-foot telephone booth–like cab with flat overhanging roof reflected the vernacular character of these early structures. These simple structures allowed sheltered views of the surrounding forest for miles.

SANTIAGO PEAK RESIDENCE, 1916. Santiago Peak was the second lookout constructed on the forest. By 1916, its original six-by-six-foot lookout cab and board-and-batten residence "shack" was supplemented with this residence. Two years after this photograph, it would also be the site of Cleveland history, when Winifred Hunter served as a seasonal guard—the first non-clerical female employee of the forest.

SECOND HOT SPRINGS LOOKOUT, C. 1932. In the early 1920s, staff replaced the original Hot Springs Lookout with the region's standard-plan 14-by-14-foot lookout providing more hospitable accommodations for the guard and, in this case, his wife. Early forest wives were not official employees, but at remote posts, they worked just as hard, and sacrificed just as much, as their Forest Service spouses.

Boucher Hill Lookout, c. 1930. Not all lookouts were standard. This water tank–style structure at Boucher Hill on Palomar Mountain, along with its small sleeping cabin, served until replaced in the mid-1930s. Such amenities did not ease guard life from substandard water systems, hauling firewood over poor trails, and duty that allowed only for monthly trips into town for supplies, entertainment, and society.

Fire Patrol Programs, 1919. The Cleveland was an experimental location for testing aircraft for fire patrol. In 1919, the Forest Service and Army Air Corps worked a cooperative agreement for its airplanes. Although promising for detection of fires, several problems, most notably lack of radio communication, ended this initial program as the live homing pigeons proved unreliable. Aircraft would later return.

GUARD SCHOOL HELIOGRAPH TRAINING, 1927. Operating a heliograph was a standard part of fireguard training. Former Cleveland supervisor S. A. "Gus" Nash-Boulden reportedly helped standardize the code for heliographs. The device used a series of mirrors to send signals long distances. The heliograph would rapidly decline in use after the arrival of portable radios in the 1930s.

ANNUAL GUARD SCHOOL, 1932. Annual fireguard school was essential training for all fire staff. Trainings took advantage of the latest information in fire studies, techniques, and experience. Forest staff worked cooperatively with various agencies, including training a crew from the Pala Indian Reservation. In the early Depression years, such as in this photograph, recruiting for the government fire jobs was less challenging.

Fire Guard Setting Backfire, 1932. As fire science and knowledge was accumulated and put into practice, new techniques and equipment were added to the firefighters' arsenal. Setting backfires to consume combustible fuels in front of fire lines was enhanced with devices such as this backpack flamethrower. Such cutting-edge techniques and equipment received extensive focus in fire-prone Southern California.

Beauty Mountain Fire, 1928. The Cleveland avoided significant fire acreage loss since the 65,000-acre Barona fire of 1913. In September 1928, the 67,000-acre Beauty Mountain, 33,240-acre Witch Creek, and 27,925-acre San Diego River fires burned more forest acreage than in the previous 15 years. The Beauty Mountain fire significantly damaged Oak Grove Station.

FIRE INVESTIGATOR, C. 1920S. All the Cleveland's severe fires of 1928 were started intentionally or accidentally. Fire control managers soon added fire investigation to their skill sets. What started as a program to better understand fire behavior soon added elements of law enforcement detective work. The resulting studies reinforced the need for additional prevention and public information efforts.

RANGER'S PATROL CAR, 1923. The Cleveland staff took advantage of all available promotional opportunities, such as this spare tire, to inform the public on fire prevention. Articles in newspapers and magazines focused on the dangers of visitors' campfires and cigarettes. In 1930, Cleveland rangers even established smoking stations and handed out free "butt bags" for depositing used cigarettes.

FOREST SERVICE INFORMATION EXHIBIT, 1918. This exhibit at the 1918 Escondido Grape Day Celebration provided the type of public outreach necessary for promoting the young service's mission, rules, and regulations. Booths at public events and fairs during this period were important opportunities to educate on fire prevention, recreational options, and watershed protection.

FLAPJACK DEMONSTRATION, 1919. Rangers interacting with the public have been, and still are, an effective tool for communicating forest rules, regulations, and recommended visitor behavior. This exhibit at the San Bernardino Fair, sponsored by the Southern California National Forests, features a realistic forest scene including a painted backdrop and campfire for Ranger J. B. Stephenson to cook pancakes.

Palomar Timber Sale, 1924. By 1912, the forest had only one active sawmill permit, located near Idyllwild on the San Jacinto. Occasional timber sales such as this one on Palomar Mountain were rare. Typically timber permits occurred to help clear disease-ridden wood or reduce fire loads.

Old Mining Claim, c. 1930. Mining was another land use that forest officers faced. Federal law allowed individuals to obtain and maintain mining claims on national forests. Although the Cuyamacas had been the scene of several 19th-century mining booms, no large-scale mining operations occurred on the forest. Most staff time on mining dealt with investigating legitimacy of claims and enforcing forest rules.

Rangers Examining Chaparral, 1915. Foresters looked to constantly learn more about the Cleveland's forest resources. Early foresters from other areas examining the Cleveland were often stumped as to how to increase timber stands. Experiments continued with new fast-growing species such as black locust and eucalyptus, although they proved ineffective to increase forest cover.

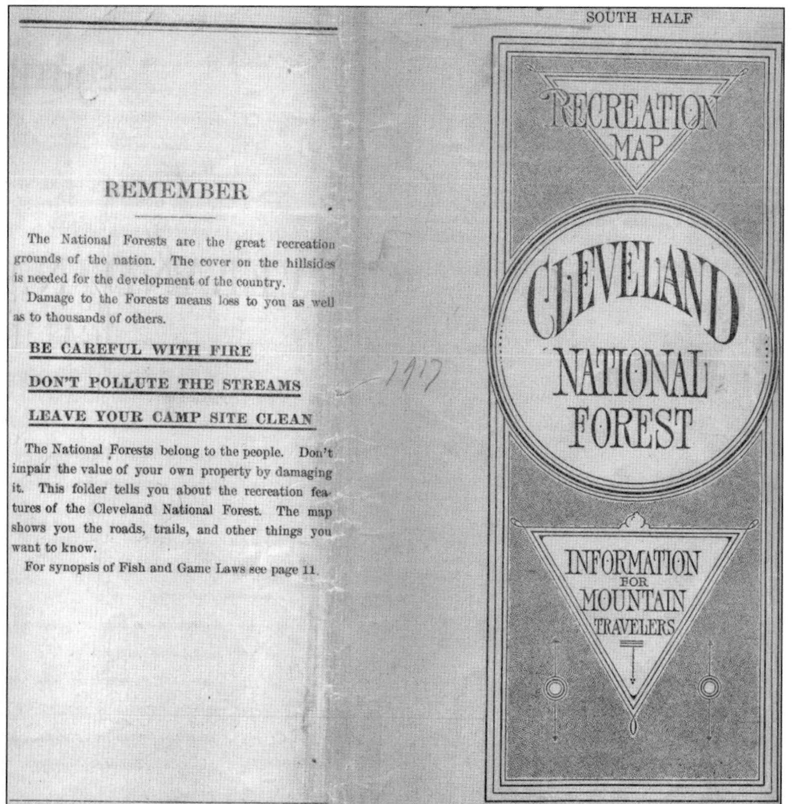

REMEMBER

The National Forests are the great recreation grounds of the nation. The cover on the hillsides is needed for the development of the country.

Damage to the Forests means loss to you as well as to thousands of others.

BE CAREFUL WITH FIRE

DON'T POLLUTE THE STREAMS

LEAVE YOUR CAMP SITE CLEAN

The National Forests belong to the people. Don't impair the value of your own property by damaging it. This folder tells you about the recreation features of the Cleveland National Forest. The map shows you the roads, trails, and other things you want to know.

For synopsis of Fish and Game Laws see page 11.

SOUTH HALF

RECREATION MAP

CLEVELAND NATIONAL FOREST

INFORMATION FOR MOUNTAIN TRAVELERS

1917

Recreation Map, 1917. Recreation was not a initial purpose of the forest reserves, and most reserves were far from urban centers, receiving few visitors outside of local hunters, stock grazers, or those from nearby mountain resorts. In 1899, Congress passed the first legislation related to recreation in the forests, allowing "permittees" to lease land for public-serving sanitariums, hotels, and resorts.

INSPECTING SPECIAL USE FACILITY, C. 1910S. Service chief Pinchot recognized the importance of the public's recreational use of the forests. In 1905, he established "special use permits" for commercial operators of "hotels, stores, mills, summer residences, and similar services when legitimate and consistent with the best interest of the reserves," such as this scout camp at Domenigoni Valley.

CAR CAMPERS AT STONE CREEK, 1923. Development of state, and later federal, highway systems and affordable, mass-produced automobiles were a major factor in opening the national forests. By 1923, the nation had over four million autos on the road, and organizations including the Automobile Club of Southern California promoted these opportunities such that in 1920, estimates reported over a million motorists camping out.

FULLER MILL CREEK CAMPGROUND, 1922. Forest planners looked to identify locations for public campgrounds such as this one in the San Jacinto District. During the 1910s and 1920s, the role of Forest Service versus the National Park Service and their preservation mission was debated. Yet over three million national forest visitors by 1918 entrenched recreation as an accepted use.

LAGUNA SPECIAL USE CABIN PERMITTEES, C. 1920S. For many, a summer cabin or second home represented an unprecedented recreational opportunity. Passage of the Occupancy Permit Act of 1915 allowed up to 30 years on a permit, increasing demand rapidly, especially in Southern California. Soon Cleveland planners laid out summer home tracts throughout the forest to meet this demand.

HULBURD SPECIAL USE TRACT, C. 1920S. Assuming summer home demand from not only rapidly urbanizing areas but also the newly settled Imperial County, forest managers initially surveyed as many as 20 different tracts on the four districts. Many became "ghost tracts" that were abandoned. Some tracts such as this one near Descanso were placed adjacent to highways and existing recreational areas.

SPECIAL USE CABIN, TRABUCO CANYON, C. 1920S. Although the Descanso District has the majority of cabins, the Trabuco District developed four tracts, the first in Trabuco Canyon. In the mid-1920s, additional small tracts at Holy Jim Canyon, San Juan, and Hot Springs were surveyed and rapidly filled. This rustic-style cabin reflects the use of local materials in designing these seasonal cabins.

LAGUNA RECREATIONAL RESIDENCE, 1923. The conveniences of summer home cabins, along with the development of roads into the formerly remote forest, provided new recreational opportunities. The original concept for "packing-in" supplies for a full summer away from home was quickly supplanted by weekend or day trips. Also unlike snowbound regions, the Cleveland tracts were generally available year-round for families to enjoy.

LAGUNA RECREATION BROCHURE, C. 1919. Rising over 5,000 feet with woodlands, open meadows, and views east to the Colorado Desert, the area had much recreational potential. District planners identified this, writing in 1912, "The Laguna Mountains make a delightful place for summer residence [for] the people of Imperial Valley and the vicinity of San Diego." The next year, a classification study confirmed recreation as the area's best use.

RANGER AT LAGUNA JUNCTION, c. 1920. The Lagunas' recreational development required safe automobile access. Early pioneers rode the rough Kitchen Creek wagon road past Flynn Ranch. Direct access was needed from the Pine Valley area. In 1918, forest supervisor S. W. Wynne secured Forest Service road funds under the promise of a revenue-producing area for the timber-revenue-sparse Cleveland.

AUTO NEGOTIATING NEW LAGUNA ROAD, 1920. The original Laguna Road construction cost $39,078.32. Supervisor Wynne compiled funding from several sources, completing a 12-foot-wide single-track road with occasional turnouts that lasted as such throughout the 1920s. Rangers controlled traffic at peak use periods to incoming vehicles in the early mornings and outgoing vehicles in the late afternoons.

LAGUNA (EL PRADO) CAMPGROUND, C. 1920. Funds for campground improvements and facilities were minimal. By summer 1922, only three campgrounds were open, including the Laguna, Boiling Springs, and Verde. The Laguna Campground was the most developed, with four latrines, six tables and benches, three incinerators, three garbage pits, and two wells.

BURNT RANCHERIA CAMPGROUND, C. 1925. Visitor numbers continued to increase as locals learned of the Lagunas' recreational opportunities. Forest managers made cooperative arrangements to construct facilities such as Burnt Rancheria, opened in 1924. The Automobile Club of Southern California provided funds to help rangers construct the new campground to accommodate the nearly 1,000 monthly visitors to the Lagunas.

LAGUNA RECREATION AREA FIRE ALARM, C. 1925. With thousands of visitors camping, picnicking, and hiking throughout the Laguna area, fire prevention and suppression were a main concern. This alarm was also funded through donations, in this case from the City of La Mesa in 1924, and signaled all available men to report for fire duty.

LAGUNA RECREATION AREA GATE, C. 1926. On September 24, 1926, the Secretary of Agriculture formally established the 11,495-acre Laguna Mountain Recreation Area. Forester L. A. Barrett reiterated that as "this tract is the only one of its kind anywhere in the extreme southern end of the state and is visited by thousands of people annually, it should be permanently dedicated to recreational use."

SHRINE CAMP LODGE BUILDING, 1927. In addition to public campgrounds and summer homes, several service groups and organizations obtained special use permits for lodges and camps. In 1922, San Diego's Al Bahr Shriners Lodge obtained leases to the El Prado Summer Home Tract, building a small clubhouse in 1923. In 1926–1927, forest supervisor Joe Elliott helped survey 18 additional lots to the north for new cabins and a lodge building. Elliott also provided construction oversight to assist in building the large lodge hall. The Shriners Lodge is the largest special use structure on the forest and still provides the Shriners with a rustic mountain setting for their gatherings. Although remodeled and upgraded, the rustic architecture featuring stone fireplace and exposed log beams still exists.

LAGUNA RESORT AND KEHOE'S LODGE, C. 1920S. In addition, several commercial operations also provided public services. In 1919, G. L. "Doc" Terry opened a store and eating house known as the Laguna Resort in the Burnt Rancheria tract to serve both day visitors and campers. William Kehoe's Blue Jay Lodge opened a year or two later across the road and provided a store and small cottages for travelers. Soon Fisk's Store and Salisbury's Resorts also provided food, supplies, and lodging for Laguna visitors. Special uses also included Frank Session's "saddle livery" in the El Centro tract, providing horses and tack for visitors. During the same time, a service station and store opened at the Laguna Junction along the newly designated U.S. 80 at Laguna Summit.

Campfire Girls at Clubhouse, c. 1920s. By the mid-1920s, "group camps" and cabins or clubhouses had been permitted for the Imperial Valley YMCA, Southwestern Baptist Association, Methodist Church, 4-H Club, and San Diego Girl Scouts. Here a group of Campfire Girls enjoys a visit in front of the Girl Scouts clubhouse.

Game-Refuge Sign, c. 1920s. As early as 1925, rangers documented decreases in small game compared to previous decades. Large game animal reduction prompted enforcement against illegal hunting. Ironically from today's perspective, as the forest staff practiced cutting-edge ecological methods such as reintroducing a small elk herd to the Lagunas, the forest simultaneously employed a full-time "stalker" to hunt mountain lions and coyotes.

AGUA TIBIA PRIMITIVE AREA, C. 1930S. In the 1920s, foresighted Forest Service employees such as ranger/writer Aldo Leopold and landscape architect Arthur Carhart introduced the idea of designating undeveloped "primitive areas." Cleveland supervisor Joseph Elliott identified roughly 35,000 "wild" acres in the Agua Tibia Range north of Palomar Mountain. In 1931, the Agua Tibia Primitive Area became the Cleveland's initial wilderness zone.

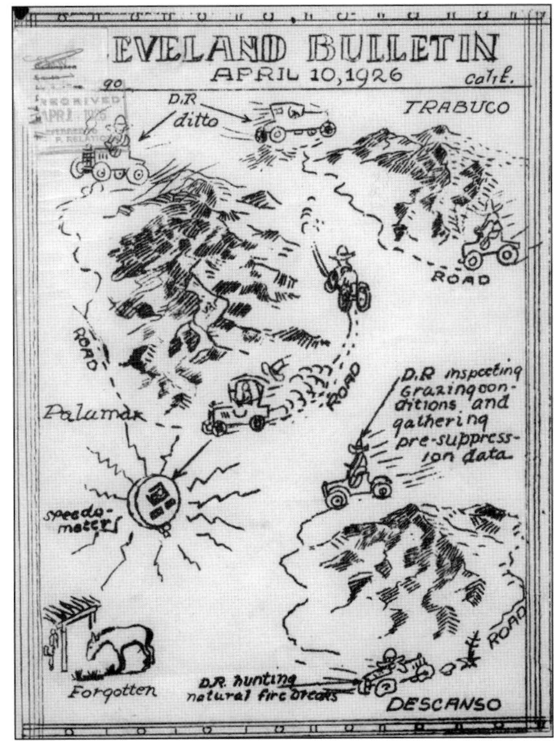

CHANGING TIMES FOR RANGERS. This 1926 cover of the *Cleveland Bulletin* employee newsletter indicated not only a good-natured poking of fun at management, but one of the most influential changes affecting Cleveland's rangers—the automobile. The horse at the bottom left, once the most important piece of ranger "equipment," was now regulated to backcountry travels and recreational rides.

RANGER ROAD TRIP, 1932. From left to right, Rangers Toveil, Christenson, and Fromboe undertake a wildlife survey from their rumble-seat roadster. Roads, truck trails, and autos helped "shrink" the forest for staff. At the same, these roads, trails, and recreational facilities had opened the forest to what were now well over one million Southern California residents—threefold more than at forest establishment in 1908.

FOREST ROAD WORK CREW, C. 1925. Early forest managers rarely received funding to undertake large, labor-intensive engineering and construction projects such as building the Corona-Black Star road shown here. Thus, when the stock market crashed in October 1929 and the United States rapidly slipped into the Great Depression, an already understaffed and under-financed Cleveland could not foresee the positive changes forthcoming.

Three

A New Deal for Growth 1933–1941

In the 1930s, the Forest Service and the Cleveland National Forest experienced their greatest period of development. Although the nation was in its worst economic depression ever, the Forest Service effectively took advantage of Pres. Franklin Delano Roosevelt's New Deal programs, specifically the Civilian Conservation Corps (CCC), to expand and develop forest infrastructure. Forest Service personnel instructed and directed CCC enrollees, along with other relief program laborers, to construct much-needed administrative buildings and improvements, including residences, guard stations and lookouts, erosion structures, roads, trails and firebreaks, and camping and recreation facilities. For the Cleveland National Forest, the New Deal period experienced an over 100-percent increase in these facilities and improvements. Additionally, with over 275,000 people within a two-hour drive of the forest in San Diego County alone and the construction of new roads and highways, such as the completion of the Ortega Highway across the Santa Ana Mountains in 1933, the forest was open to public use as never before. The Cleveland managers' focus toward watershed and fire management that dominated forest policy now began to emphasize recreation, mimicking the new service-wide focus. The California region subsequently directed recreational planning, providing standardized designs for administrative and recreational sites similar to the Park Rustic design program that the National Park Service had developed in the 1920s. The United States' entry into World War II in December 1941 abruptly ended this period of unprecedented growth and development. Although the regional forester had painted a grim picture of the Depression-era service in 1931, the New Deal funding and labor provided Cleveland staff with the opportunity to meet the underlying watershed management goals of the forest through unprecedented infrastructure development. It also allowed the Cleveland to adopt modern firefighting, engineering, and recreation techniques and policies. Although range, mining, and land management concerns still were management factors, the New Deal era entrenched the regionally significant focus toward recreational use for the forest. As the Cleveland entered World War II, the foundations for the modern-era forest had been set in place.

SERA WORKERS' PAYDAY, 1933. In fall 1931, Gov. James Rolph created a Labor Camp Committee to establish work camps for California's unemployed men. The Forest Service, as well as state and local agencies, was assigned to operate and conduct the camps. The Cleveland operated State Employment Relief Administration (SERA) camps at Trabuco Canyon in 1931–1932 and at Temescal, Guatay, and Laguna in 1932–1933.

SERA WORK CREW, 1933. Regional forester Stuart Bevier Show recognized that such labor programs could prove beneficial to California's national forests. In 1933, Show became an important advocate for newly elected Pres. Franklin Roosevelt's proposed federal Civilian Conservation Corps program. Therefore, on April 21, 1933, Show received orders to begin preparation for over 60 CCC camps immediately.

CCC CAMP PORTRAIT, 1937. On March 31, 1933, Congress passed Roosevelt's Emergency Conservation Work (ECW) program "for the relief of unemployment through performance of useful public work." The Civilian Conservation Corps (CCC) was the agency created to implement such conservation work. The CCC recruited young men between the ages of 18 and 25 from throughout the nation to work in 200-man corps for six-month enrollment periods.

CAMP MINNEWAWA NEAR JAMUL, 1933. By end of June 1933, the Cleveland had eight new CCC Camps. Early camps consisted of platform tent barracks with only a few wooden prefabricated army buildings for mess halls, kitchens, and utility buildings. The average time for initial camp construction was just 12 to 15 days.

DISTRICT COMMANDER INSPECTION, CAMP TEMECULA, 1933. With their expertise in training and managing large numbers of young men, CCC camp administration was assigned to the U.S. Army. Army officers commanded each camp, and buildings and layouts were designed to accommodate groups of 210 enrollees who were required to adhere to army discipline and regulations.

CNF STAFF, CAMP TEMESCAL, 1933. Forest supervisor Louis Anderson is on the left with Trabuco District rangers. In April, Anderson ordered equipment transferred from the state relief camps to sites at Temescal and Pine Valley. On May 13, Camp Pine Valley became the first CCC camp to open in California. Camps Temescal, Pamo, Temecula, Puerta La Cruz, Santee, Fallbrook, and Lyons Valley soon followed.

TRENCH WORK, CAMP TEMESCAL, 1933. The CCC enrollees helped build their own camps using an advance group of 20 to 25 enrollees to set up the initial tent camp. Under Army Corps officers, the full corps cleared the site, dug latrines, and installed the water system. Then with direction from local carpenters and plumbers, "experienced men," they would construct the wood-frame buildings.

KITCHEN CREW, CAMP TEMECULA, 1938. Early on, a small number of African American men were enrolled in the CCC. However, in 1930s America, an integrated program was not the official CCC policy. After several incidents at camps nationwide, the army ordered camps segregated. The Cleveland Forest had two such segregated camps, at Elsinore's La Cienega and at Camp Minnewawa near Jamul.

SAWMILL WORKER, CAMP PINE VALLEY, 1934. Paying $25 a month, $20 of which was sent home to dependants, the CCC also offered recruits occupational and educational programs. The program hired "local experienced men" to provide CCC enrollees skilled training. Camp Pine Valley, for example, included modern training facilities such as a blacksmith shop, woodshop, photographic darkroom, and classrooms.

CAMP LA CIENEGA'S "BROWN BOMBERS," 1937. Recreational activities were also available, and most camps had ball fields, basketball hoops, and/or gyms and boxing rings. Camp Pine Valley had its own quarter-mile track; tennis, badminton, and volleyball courts; and a small nine-hole golf course. La Cienega's camp basketball team poses here for a photograph after winning their second consecutive Southern California district championship.

SUPERVISOR ELLIS AND STAFF, C. 1935. In late 1934, former Angeles NF assistant Guerdon Ellis (first row, left) became supervisor. Ellis administered significant modernization of the Cleveland operations. Here Ellis poses with key forest staff, from left to right, (first row) J. B. Stephenson, Descanso District; (second row) Hayward Fletcher, Palomar District; C. M. Gwin, executive assistant; Ina Wright, clerk; and Virgil DeLapp, Trabuco District.

FORESTER SHOW WITH SOCAL SUPERVISORS, 1936. Guerdon Ellis's three-year tenure included significant coordination with the other Southern California forest supervisors. Ellis is shown here at a meeting with regional forester Stuart Show (first row, center) and, from left to right, (second row) Los Padres's Harve Roberts, future CNF supervisor Antonio Dean, former supervisor Gus Nash-Boulden of the San Bernardino, unidentified, and the Angeles's Bill Mendenhall.

Office and Barracks, Corona, 1938. California's national forests took advantage of the deep labor pool and funding opportunities to develop building and improvement programs previously unfathomed. Show authorized hiring professional architects Blanchard and Maher and landscape architects Hall and Gibbs to prepare plans for new buildings and sites. These professional designers created a standard style for the region they described as "Mother Lode" architecture.

Construction of Corona Warehouse, 1933. Blanchard and Maher identified 13 different building types needed to serve sites of varied uses, climates, and elevations, including residences, fire and guard stations, warehouses, garages, water towers, pump and power houses, and fire lookouts. Building cost limitations forced development of wooden "ready-cut" construction methods using prefabricated and mass-produced standard hardware, trusses, and lumber.

PALA GUARD STATION, 1938. Landscape architect L. Glenn Hall also pioneered standards for design of administrative and recreational sites. Hall developed a landscape manual outlining site design objectives complementary of Blanchard and Maher's work: rugged simplicity and naturalness, adaptation to surrounding landscape, and minimal costs. This Pala Guard Station layout is typical of Hall's understated and functional site designs.

PALOMAR OBSERVATORY GUARD STATION, 1938. By 1940, the Cleveland had directed construction of new standard-plan guard stations at Alpine, Cameron Valley, Laguna (Camp Ole), Pine Hills, Henshaw, Pala, Tenaja, El Cariso, Trabuco, Silverado, Temecal, and Palomar. Only the Observatory Guard Station on the road to Cal Tech's under-construction Palomar Observatory received special Mediterranean Revival architectural details and styling.

RANGER HAYWARD'S FAMILY, 1938. An August 1934 *San Diego Union* article headlined "Depression gives Forest Rangers Roof Over Heads." Supervisor Anderson noted how the modern, convenient, and practical designs of the new residence structures with their pine interiors, built-in cupboards, coolers (refrigerators), and sinks provided significant upgrades for staff—such as Palomar District ranger Fletcher Hayward and family.

PALOMAR (HIGH POINT) LOOKOUT, 1935. CCCs also helped forest staff erect other new administrative sites such as fire lookouts. Five new metal-frame stations were completed, including ones at Black Mountain, Estelle Peak, Santa Margarita, Silverado Peak, and Palomar Mountain (later known as High Point). The five new lookouts brought the forest total to 11, providing comprehensive viewpoint coverage.

CCC BUILDING TRUCK TRAIL, 1934. Early in the program, the CCC was assigned to construct many roads, firebreaks, and trails. Crews spent significant time using shovels, picks, and dig-bars to cut road and trail beds from the rugged hills and slopes. Truck trails and firebreaks provided important access for firefighting and prevention work into previously inaccessible areas of the forest.

PREPARING BLASTING HOLE, 1934. CCC enrollees were also provided training in more skilled tasks. Large boulders and outcrops often required removal via dynamite. Here a young enrollee digs a dynamite hole to remove and loosen a large rock outcrop during construction of the Barber Truck Trail. Such skills, although dangerous, provided select young men expertise for future employment.

BUILDING PALOMAR HIGHWAY, 1937. The Cleveland's CCC crews also assisted with the building of several key roads in and around the forest, including the "Highway to the Stars" on Palomar Mountain and the Sunrise Highway extension connecting the Lagunas to Lake Cuyamaca. These crews also helped with construction of highway bridges on state, federal, and county roads in and around the forest.

EAGLE TRUCK TRAIL, 1934. Records indicate that the CCC crews, along with other New Deal labor programs such as the Civil Works Administration (CWA), helped construct nearly 1,000 miles of truck trails, firebreaks, and roads on the Cleveland—many still in use today. This improvement work also provided the impetus for hiring the first staff civil engineers for the forest.

Ranger Measuring Erosion, 1939. Rangers worked with engineering professionals on erosion issues. Here a ranger measures the effectiveness of erosion control structures in holding soils along a steep bank of the Santiago Fire Break on the Trabuco District. Forest service erosion experts worked on watershed protection issues both on and off the Cleveland in order to improve the region's water-retention capabilities.

Sheephead Erosion Project, 1940. One of the great concerns for forest managers was erosion in areas cleared of brush from fire or overgrazing. In an effort to reduce the transport of valuable soils and the subsequent drop of the water table, the CCC erected hundreds of erosion control structures such as this stone check-dam in the Laguna Mountains.

GUARD SCHOOL TRAINING SESSION, 1938. Fire was still the Cleveland's number one threat. Taking advantage of the California region's groundbreaking efforts in fire control, behavior, and science, the annual fire guard schools continued to provide CNF staff with the latest in fire management knowledge. Fireguards were also provided with a new *Region 5 Fire Manual* implementing cutting-edge policies and tactics.

CCC FIRE SUPPRESSION TRAINING, 1933. Hundreds of able-bodied and trained fire crews allowed for implementation and evaluation of the newest firefighting and prevention practices, including post-fire revegetation and erosion control work. By 1937, the newly appointed Regional Fire Management officer, R. W. Ayres, remarked on the invaluable role that the CCC crews provided in advancing the fire control program.

WEATHER STATION, 1937, AND DRY-ICE TANKER, 1937. Technology and innovation were hallmarks of the New Deal-era fire program. Research into the connection between weather conditions and fire behavior helped institute the daily routine of weather recordation, such as shown above at the box weather stations that became standard equipment at all guard stations. In addition, technological innovations such as the "dry ice" tanker system in the photograph below would provide precedent for later chemical suppression systems. Although this particular system never proved significantly field effective, the funding and staff levels of the period provided fire managers the opportunity to creatively experiment and improve their programs with such innovations.

EL CARISO TANKER TRUCK, 1937. A fleet of new tanker trucks along with the thousands of miles of new firebreaks, truck trails, and roads allowed suppression crews to attack fires early. The added staffing, equipment, and cooperation of state and local agencies helped the Cleveland with record low burned acreage years, including just 42 acres burned in 27 events in 1937.

SILVERADO CANYON SUPPRESSION CREW, 1935. Guard station suppression crews became the key firefighting units. Each station was assigned a permanent crew captain, complemented with seasonal firefighters. The pride of each station was its tanker truck. The Dodge Brothers "lightweight" model shown here was the most common make used on the Cleveland during this period, serving well into the 1940s.

FIRE DISPATCHER MILLER, 1938. Fire management modernization instituted a centralized communication program. In addition to a forest fire management officer, the forest also added permanent fire dispatchers. Here Dispatcher Clare Miller charts a fire from Oak Grove. Such communication systems connected fire lookouts, stations, field crews, and patrol aircraft via radio.

CCC CREWMAN WITH RADIO, 1940. Radio communication was another key for fire management modernization. Supervisor Guerdon Ellis made establishment of a radio communication system a forest priority before his transfer to the Trinity National Forest in late 1936. For fire management, this "stand-by" or portable radio was key to connecting fire crews to fire command.

Palomar Fire from Aircraft, 1934. Using aircraft for fire patrol was revived in the early 1930s. Regional contracts provided for a single airplane to scout large fires in Southern California. Although the Forest Service experimented with fighting fire from the air, it would not be realized until after World War II. However, radio institutionalized the scouting value of aircraft.

Packaging Goods for Air Drop, c. 1938. Dropping supplies to remote locations was another use of aircraft in the 1930s. In an effort to protect the goods, they were bundled, padded, and given burlap parachutes to reduce the impact. This photograph shows preparations for packing supplies for a test drop from March Army Air Field in Riverside County.

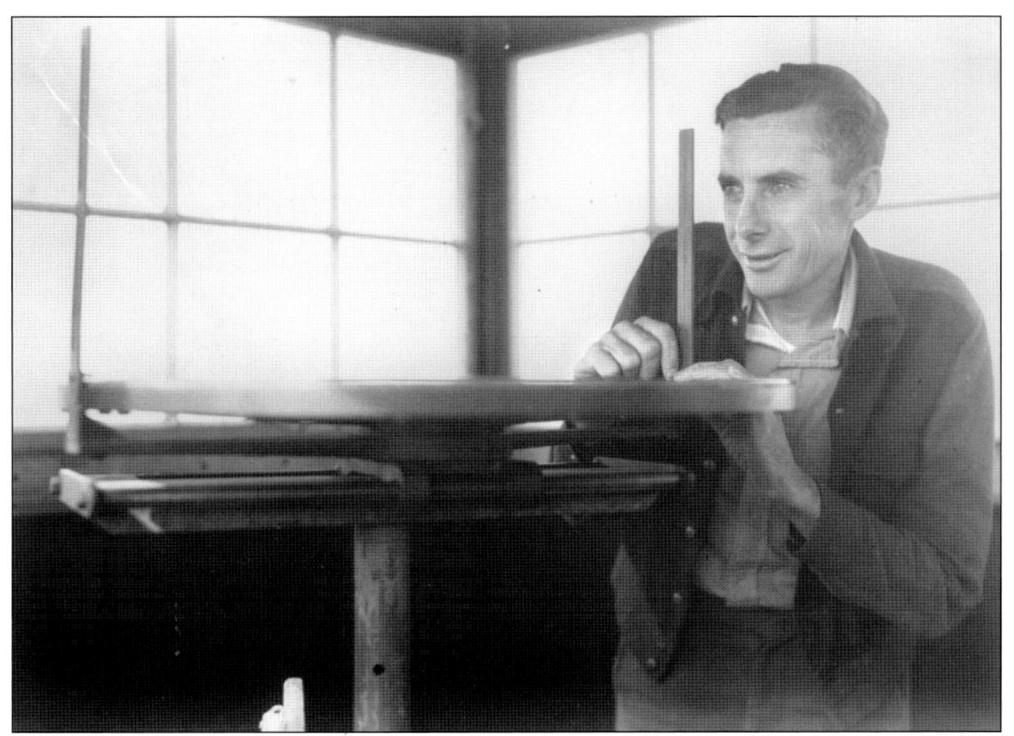

LOOKOUT DEMONSTRATING FIRE FINDER, 1935. The effectiveness of fire detection systems also increased in the 1930s. One of the key pieces to the success of fire detection was the Osbourne Fire Finder. The Fire Finder had been invented in the 1910s, and from the 1920s to 1935, they were required lookout equipment, allowing for accurate locating of fires.

PAMO FIRE CAMP, 1935. Combining communications, detailed weather and wind data, accessibility throughout the forest, more stations, equipment, and CCC labor, all had to be strategically coordinated. Field fire camps were essential to this coordination. Forest staff became experts in quickly establishing fire camps wherever needed to provide rapid and effective management of fire events.

ADMINISTRATIVE STAFF AT PAMO FIRE CAMP, 1935. From wives of early rangers to lookout guards to office support and beyond, women have fulfilled valued roles in the Forest Service. Here two female employees provide administrative support at fire camp. Fire management coordination, including recording costs and tracking supplies and equipment, created large amounts of paperwork and administrative need for competent, adaptive, and skilled employees.

FIRE DESTROYED TANKER TRUCK, 1938. Even with modern fire management, the unpredictability of wildfires made suppression activities dangerous. This photograph shows the results of the power and speed of fire surges such as the one that overtook this tanker truck. Luckily this fire did not injure any firefighters; such luck would not always be the case.

Fire Prevention Sign, c. 1930s. Forest Service public relations continued to focus on fire prevention. Signage helped with voluntary compliance as well as regulatory enforcement. This sign, located along the forest boundary on the Ortega Highway on the Riverside County side, provided posting of the supervisor's fire prevention orders, often closing the forest during high fire danger periods.

Display, Marston's Store, San Diego, 1938. Cleveland staff under new supervisor Andrew Brenneis developed this public education exhibit for the forest's 30th anniversary. At age 30, Brenneis was the youngest supervisor named to lead the Cleveland. The Penn State forestry school graduate's two-year tenure was marked by openness to technological advancements such as his interest in aviation.

EXHIBITS AT CALIFORNIA-PACIFIC INTERNATIONAL EXPOSITION, 1935. One of the most fondly remembered public relations efforts of the New Deal era was the exhibit at the 1935–1936 California-Pacific Exposition at Balboa Park in San Diego. The exhibit included both the traditional educational and public information displays on the Cleveland and Forest Service's mission, recreational opportunities, and fire prevention programs—and a complete CCC camp with buildings, structures, and tanker trucks. Identified as Camp San Diego, the full-scale camp exhibit included a full complement of enrollees who provided demonstrations of forestry skills and improvement work.

TRABUCO DISTRICT DEMONSTRATION, 1938. District ranger A. M. Longacre (with watering cans) and a ranger demonstrate the difference between erosion of vegetated soils and non-vegetated soils. This homemade demonstration device helped explain the need for forest cover in protecting the watershed of the Cleveland. Such public events provided visitors a mixture of education and entertainment, as well as an opportunity to meet forest staff.

FOREST HOMESTEAD SITE, 1935. Uses such as grazing, timber, and mining provided smaller concerns. However, a relatively high amount of staff time was spent in investigating fraudulent mining and land claims that were illegally used for residences, agriculture, or summer cabins. Regional surveyor William "Ole" Friedhoff reported that the Forest Service contested well more than half of the region's claims during this period.

CCC CREW PLANTING TREE, 1941. Managing timbering activities was also minimal. By the mid-1930s, timber removal permits were limited to small wood-cutting operators. Foresters used CCC labor with replanting work and fuel reduction projects. Previously controversial prescribed or "light-burning" was reconsidered but still not formally accepted for Forest Service policy in this period.

BAJA CALIFORNIA TRIP, 1937. Forest staff often provided cooperative efforts with other federal agencies in pioneering wildlife management programs. In the late 1930s, staff joined Dr. Paul R. Needham of the U.S. Bureau of Fisheries on trips to the Rio San Domingo in Baja California, Mexico. Here Needham aerates the tank water for transporting collected fish back for propagation and restocking California waterways.

RANGER WITH BOBCAT CUBS, 1937. Forest managers made wildlife management a focus after cooperating with the California State Game Commission in establishing state game reserves in the 1910s. By the 1930s, wildlife management was one of the key elements in the "Multiple-Purpose Management" goals that would become the mantra of the postwar modern-era Forest Service, introducing the foundation for future natural resource programming.

BURNT RANCHERIA CAMPGROUND, 1937. Automobiles and new roads increased access to the forest and subsequently the number of visitors. The demand resulted in the development of new campgrounds, picnic areas, trails, and visitor services facilities. By 1937, the CNF Recreational Plan indicated that forest managers recognized recreation, right behind watershed projection, for use of the Cleveland's lands.

Laguna Campground Kiosk, 1940. Regional architects Blanchard and Maher also designed standard-plan structures for recreation. Typical standard recreational facility structures included kiosks, comfort stations, shower combination buildings, and visitor contact stations. CCC labor also provided the muscle for constructing these rustic-style buildings along with other recreational structures such as bridges, fencing, retaining walls, and water and sewer infrastructure systems.

"Klamath-Style" Camp Stove, 1934. Regional landscape architect L. Glenn Hall also designed numerous structures in support of recreational facilities. Some of the most iconic of the "park rustic"–style structures constructed were the stone masonry "Klamath" camp stoves. These stoves were named for the Klamath National Forest and sometimes were also referred to as "Lassen" stoves.

UPPER SAN JUAN CAMPGROUND, 1940. The opening of the Ortega Highway provided access to the previously remote Trabuco District mountains. CCC labor helped construct three new campgrounds along the highway: El Cariso and Upper and Lower San Juan. An additional campground was built at Tenaja on the east side of the district as well as improvements to existing facilities in Trabuco, Silverado, and San Juan Canyons.

FLOOD DAMAGE, TRABUCO CANYON, 1937. As early as 1920, forest managers considered establishing Trabuco Canyon as a recreational area. By the mid-1930s, four campgrounds and 74 recreational cabins had been developed. The winter 1937–1938 floods, however, caused severe damage, destroying cabins in both Trabuco and Holy Jim Canyons, washing out two camping areas and the road into the canyon.

LAGUNA ROAD IMPROVEMENTS, 1935. Although widened and paved in 1931, the Laguna Road's extension from Laguna Resort north to the Descanso to Julian Highway above Lake Cuyamaca was not completed until September 1937. In November 1937, Arthur Howell of La Mesa won the road-naming contest with his entry of "Sunrise Highway."

COTTAGES AT MOUNT LAGUNA LODGE, 1935. The new roads provided faster and safer access to the recreation area. Many new recreational "summer" residences were constructed, and the two main commercial resorts, Terry's Mount Laguna Lodge and Kehoe's Blue Jay Lodge, developed successful operations catering to visitors year-round. Terry's cabins, shown here, provided alternatives to the three Forest Service campgrounds.

FISK'S STORE, MOUNT LAGUNA, 1935. Other permittees provided services to Laguna visitors such as Fisk's Store. Fisk's provided groceries, supplies, and gasoline, and hosted the post office. Salisbury's Resort provided rental cabins, as did Lash's Store and Rentals. The Al Bahr Shriners developed their own recreational residence tract to go with their clubhouse, as did other service groups such as the 4-H Club.

BOULDER OAKS RESORT AND STORE, C. 1940. The Cleveland provided recreational facilities and services throughout San Diego's backcountry. Along U.S. 80, gas stations, motor hotels, and resorts such as at Beulah Camp, Boulder Oaks, and Laguna Junction supplemented private resorts surrounding the forest. Other public camps included Descanso's Guatay, Pine Valley, Descanso, Glencliff, Boulder Oaks and Palomar's Oak Grove, Crestline, San Luis Rey River, and Black Canyon.

SKIERS AT MOUNT LAGUNA, 1931. High elevation areas such as Mount Laguna provided winter sports. Cleveland managers had big visions for winter sports development, but the inconsistency and volume of snow derailed these ideas. The lack of severe weather, however, did provide year-round recreation such as hiking, swimming, fishing, hunting, and horseback riding.

LAGUNA DESERT OVERLOOK, VIEW SOUTH, 1937. The last CCC camp on the Cleveland National Forest closed in 1942. The government's funding and the political support for the New Deal programs of the 1930s waned as defense industries built up. Still, the program had provided support for regional and Cleveland managers to take chances and implement programs that would have been unfathomable for their predecessors.

Four

Multiple Uses for a Modern Forest 1941–1970

The United States' number one concern in December 1941 was no longer the Depression but World War II. The large-scale national defense and military buildup in the two years prior to the war brought about great expenditures and many new jobs. The call for manpower for national defense and military service eliminated the great need for government "make-work" programs. From 1941 to 1945, the focus of the nation's energies was on fighting and winning the war. As such, the Forest Service's improvement and recreation needs dropped rapidly on the government priority lists. Wartime demand on forest products, however, challenged many of the Forest Service policies toward resource management. War and defense industry needs stretched the Forest Service's limits in conserving forest resources. Since it was not a timber forest, the pressure on the Cleveland National Forest during the war was different. The Cleveland's emphasis on watershed protection intensified because of the rapidly growing number of military installations and war industries that ballooned San Diego County's population during the war. San Diego's growth trend would continue, as would the rest of Southern California, in the postwar period. The previously agriculture-dominated counties of Orange and Riverside would experience the same massive urbanization in the decades after the war. The huge population increases overwhelmed the watershed potential of the coastal and transverse ranges and required the importation of increasingly larger quantities of water from the Colorado River and Northern California. Although this de-emphasized the watershed component of the forest in the decades after the war, the population expansion reiterated the recreational and environmental land management needs of the region. As such, in 1960, after a decade of increasing public concern with land-use policies such as large-scale timber harvesting, Congress passed the Multiple-Use Sustained-Yield Act, the first of a wave of environmental protection laws that codified the Forest Service's commitment to management of non-timber resources and uses. As the 1960s brought societal changes nationally through civil rights and the environmental movement, the Forest Service would also adapt through multiple-use planning efforts to new legislation on wilderness, recreation, and other environmentally focused programs.

Youthful Tanker Truck Crew, 1944. Forest supervisor Norman Farrell faced a new crisis when the United States entered World War II. With only one CCC camp open, Farrell wrote a confidential report on December 3, 1941, to the regional forester of his concerns for keeping the forest open to the public with so little resources. Subsequently, the Cleveland was under a supervisor's closure order during the war.

Barona AWS Station, 1943. With the U.S. entry into World War II four days after Farrell's report, the Cleveland joined the national defense program to protect against fire sabotage. Staff cooperated with local military and civil defense organizations such as the Aircraft Warning Service (AWS) to allow use of fire lookouts and locations for observation, such as this temporary station near Barona.

World War II Fire Camp Training, 1943. Cooperation with the military included leasing of the Pine Valley CCC Camp to the Marine Corps and allowing the U.S. cavalry from Camp Lockett in Campo to train in the forest. In exchange, the forest worked to train troops for fire protection with the hope of covering the lack of available staff and labor.

Hauser Creek Fire Inquiry, 1943. World War II military firefighting support turned tragic in this October 1943 fire. Even with an experienced Forest Service crew leader, high brush and strong, unpredictable Santa Ana winds proved deadly when a sudden wind change in the box-canyon overtook the crew, killing 10 marines and 1 soldier and injuring 15, reiterating the need for improved fire safety training.

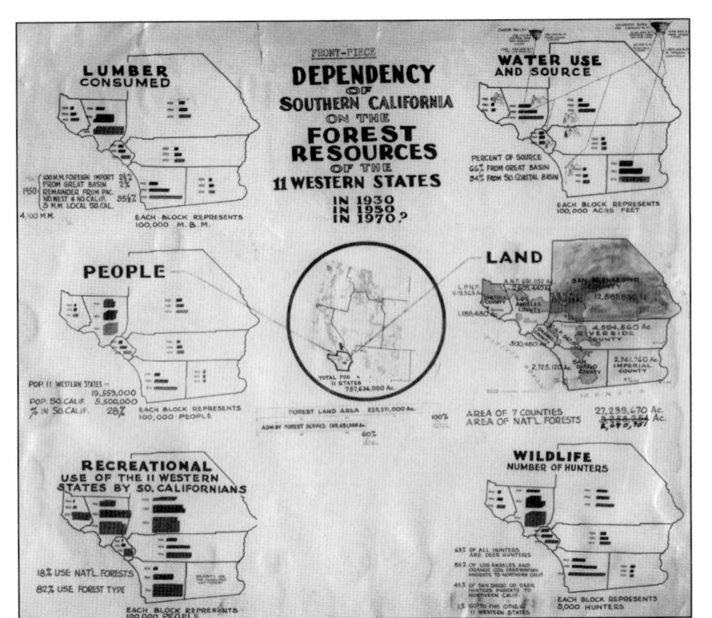

SoCal NF Multiple-Use Diagram, 1952. Multiple-use management was introduced in the 1930s, but it wasn't until after the war that multiple-use became the service's guiding policy. A 1952 Regional Task Force reported on the Southern California national forests' unique situation toward fire, recreation, and resource needs responding to exponential population growth and urban development of the region's "shrinking wildlands."

Forest Management Staff, 1967. Forest supervisor Stanley Stevenson (second row, third from right) became the stabilizing force for the Cleveland's administration. Stevenson served the longest tenure as supervisor (1957–1971). Stevenson helped transition the Cleveland from the fire-focused early 1950s into the multiple-use and sustained-yield period of the 1960s—and its new reliance on technical professionals of many disciplines.

Goose Valley Station, Ramona, 1963. After World War II, regional architect Keplar Johnson began to introduce modern and contemporary styling into new administrative structures. In addition, experiments in semi-portable and mass-produced structures resulted in a move away from the rustic styles that did not fit the new "modern" Forest Service with its emphasis on engineered and research-focused management.

Escondido Station Shop Building, c. 1960. Escondido served as Palomar District Office from 1950 to 1988, when replaced by Goose Valley. Palomar District had been considered a candidate for consolidation into the other districts until 1952 when the Pine Hills area was added to its boundaries. In the Trabuco, the DO was headquartered in rapidly growing Orange County at Santa Ana from 1960 to 1983 before returning to Corona.

ROAD DAMAGE, 1955, AND CONSTRUCTING DRAINAGE DEVICE, C. 1964. The thousands of miles of firebreaks, trails, and roads developed during the New Deal era required regular maintenance, including on occasion, significant engineering solutions. In addition, major programs for erosion control to protect soils, water, timber, wildlife, and forage in the multiple-use era also directed forest managers to hire experts. As such, the Cleveland needed new staffs of professional specialists such as civil engineers. Although it was difficult for some of the former generalist rangers to accept, these specialists helped create long-term public works solutions to troublesome site conditions and inherent problems often previously unavailable to forest managers.

Geologist Undertaking Soil Survey, 1963. Starting in the 1950s, engineers, landscape architects, silviculturists, and engineering geologists were being added to forest staffs. Following the methods of multiple-use, these specialists were focused on gathering data to provide necessary information for forest managers. Specialists soon provided updated maps, reports, and data for use by range, mining, erosion, and resource colleagues.

Erosion Damage in Rangeland, 1952. Forest specialists began to implement data gathering into permitting practices, use regulations, and engineering solutions. Such study and data allowed managers to meet the multiple-use goals for sustained yield that would allow uses such as grazing to continue to benefit both permittees and forest.

CAMERON MULTIPLE-USE AREA, 1964. The 1960 Multiple-Use Sustained-Yield Act (MUSYA) directed the Forest Service to develop renewable resource areas and uses. The Cleveland undertook several "conversion" projects such as here at Cameron Valley. The plan included the clearing of "native scrub-brush" from a former range area to help renew grazing. Interestingly, such projects would later generate concern from the growing environmental community questioning the service's interpretation of MUSYA's goals.

EL CARISO PENNY PINES PLANTATION, 1965. Forest staff worked hard to gather support from service groups and organizations such as Boy Scouts and others to promote and participate in projects such as insect control, the Tule Spring Experimental Range, and the numerous "Penny Pines" projects that gathered corporate donations to fund plantations and planting events.

DEER BROWSEWAYS, C. 1960S. Wildlife habitat improvement projects became a regular part of the multiple-use era. Here forest resource staff cut "browseways" through heavy brush areas to provide deer and other wildlife access through heavy chaparral. Other projects included building "drinkers" to provide watering holes for wildlife in dry years and seasons. Such projects lay the foundation for future habitat and ecosystem management programs.

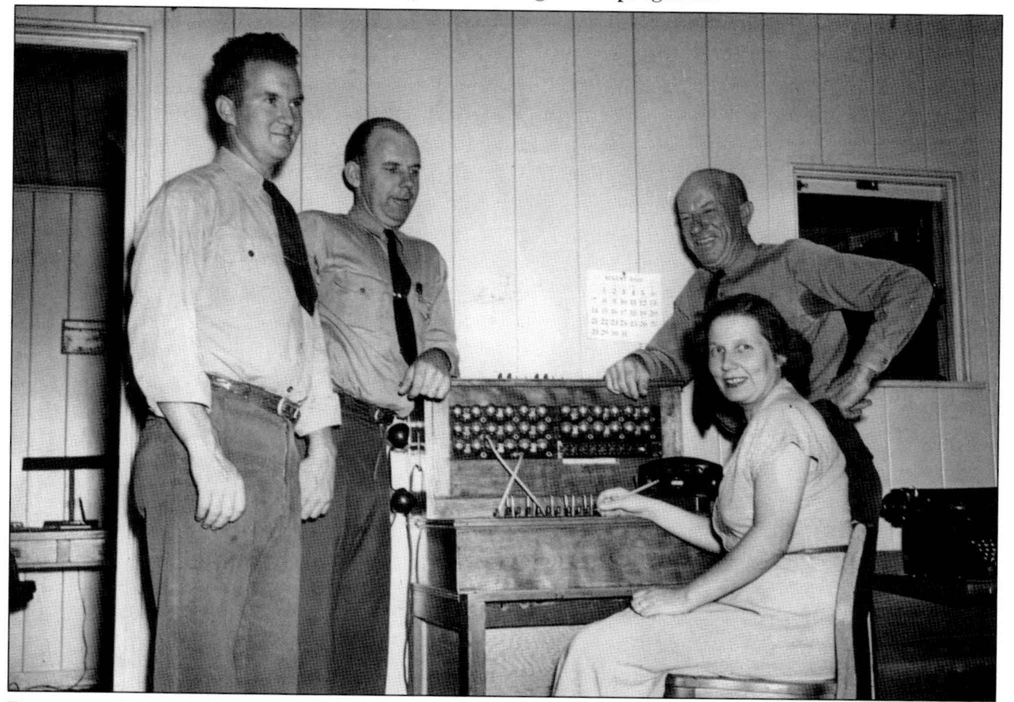

PALOMAR DISPATCH, 1949. In the 1950s, fire management dominated the Cleveland's efforts. The increase in visitors because of easier access and development into and around the forest's lands greatly increased the danger of fire. The reduced number of fire staff forced Cleveland managers to reassess their ability to respond to significant fire events.

Green River Fire, 1948. Severe fires such as the Green River fire on the Trabuco District quickly challenged Cleveland managers like Supervisor Hamilton "Ham" Pyles. Pyles and his successors would continue to push for additional staffing, equipment, and infrastructure to deal with large and threatening fires primed with heavy fuel loads accumulated from decades of suppression and no-burn policies.

Conejos Creek Fire Damage, 1950. The August 1950 fire cemented the fears of forest managers and local citizens. This fire started north of Alpine and passed east through Descanso and Cuyamaca Rancho State Park before entering Pine Valley Summer Home tract, where it destroyed 12 cabins. The 63,406-acre fire triggered a congressional investigation that brought attention—and funding—for fire control.

LAGUNA "HOT SHOTS," 1953. By 1955, Supervisor Walter Puhn noted that the fire management permanent and seasonal staffing had been raised to 133 employees. In addition, the forest created special fire "strike teams" nicknamed "Hot Shots," charged with attacking fires to reach containment as soon as possible. El Cariso was the first, formed in 1948, followed by the Laguna Hot Shots in 1951.

INAJA FIRE MEMORIAL DEDICATION SERVICE, 1957. Staffing was not the only answer to safe and effective fire control. In November 1956, the Inaja fire claimed the lives of 11 firefighters. The tragedy once again showed the dangers of placing firefighters on the line against powerful and unpredictable wildfires. This event, along with other tragic events, pushed the region to improve fire management training, equipment, and policies.

FIRE BEHAVIOR TRAINING, ESCONDIDO, C. 1960. Region 5 leaders responded quickly, directing forest supervisors and fire control officers to reemphasize the need for proper training in safety and fire behavior for all fire management employees. Other programs included funding for a Fire Research Laboratory in Riverside and prevention activities such as the "fuelbreak" program to replace volatile brush with lighter grasses.

LOADING COPTER FOR WATER DROP, C. 1960S. The most significant change to fire management was integration of aircraft into fire suppression. By 1950, the Forest Service in California had adapted helicopters into pinpoint aerial water bombers. Their value to non-fire work in wildlife counts, photography and mapping, law enforcement, and reseeding have made them essential parts of today's Forest Service programs.

Airplane on Aerial Drop, 1964. Water-bombing airplanes were also added to the regular fire suppression arsenal. They served as direct attack equipment, providing greater capacity for dropping water and later fire retardants. Aircraft also provided visual reconnaissance and reseeding for post-fire recovery. By 1960, the Cleveland, in coordination with the California Department of Forestry, established the Ramona Air Attack Base to provide permanent air support.

El Cariso Hot Shot Camp, c. 1965. Training, equipment, prevention work, and air support improved the safety and effectiveness of firefighting. However, the Cleveland still experienced its worst loss of life when on November 1, 1966, the El Cariso Hot Shots lost 12 firefighters at the Loop Canyon fire in Sylmar, Los Angeles County. In memoriam, the people of Sylmar renamed their public ball field for the firefighters.

Recreation Planners at Work, c. 1962. National concern for recreational opportunities on federal land pushed Congress to create the Outdoor Recreation Resources Review Commission in 1958. This coincided with the Forest Service's own Operation Outdoors five-year recreation facilities improvement program and postwar Southern California's demand for outdoor recreational facilities. From 1950 to 1960, the Cleveland experienced growth from 100,000 to 400,000 visitors annually.

APW Program Sign, Burnt Rancheria, 1963. In 1962, Congress approved the Accelerated Public Works (APW) program to provide jobs for underemployed regions. The Forest Service quickly hired over 900 employees region-wide. The Cleveland focused its nearly $400,000 allotment to help rehabilitate existing facilities and build new ones such as campgrounds, picnic areas, overlooks, highway wayside rest stops, visitor information centers, and trails.

NEW OBSERVATORY CAMPGROUND, 1963. The forest used its funds to build new facilities, such as the Observatory Campground on Palomar Mountain and the El Prado and Horse Heaven Group Camps and Agua Dulce Campground in the Laguna Recreation Area. The rest of the funds went for rehabilitation work at existing facilities forest-wide.

DEER SEASON OPENING DAY, C. 1960. Other recreational opportunities such as hunting and fishing continued to be popular during the modern era. Forest resources and wildlife specialists worked with local State Fish and Game employees to assure that deer, turkeys, and other game animals were managed under the goals for sustained yield and use. Such activities would later come under scrutiny from environmental groups.

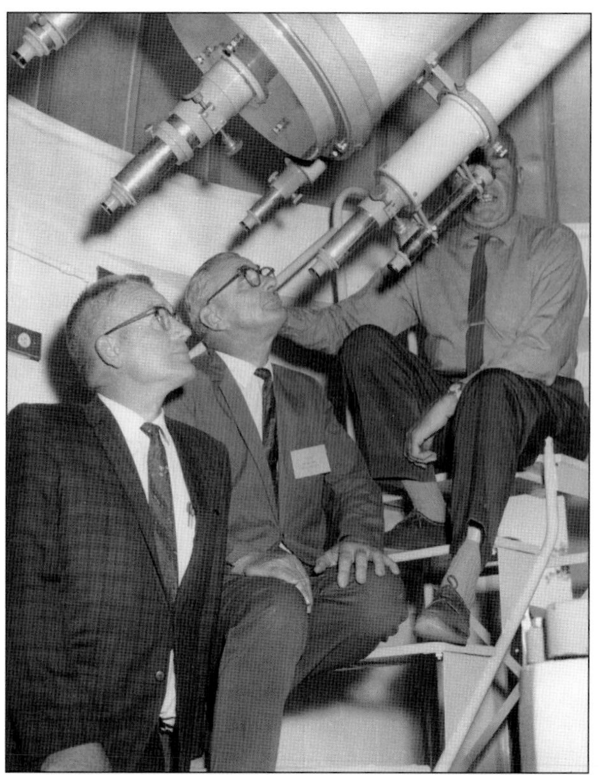

SDSC OBSERVATORY, MOUNT LAGUNA, 1968. Forest officials also continued to work cooperatively with other public institutions and organizations. In 1968, San Diego State College (SDSC) constructed a small observatory on Mount Laguna for astronomical research. Mount Laguna provided a rural refuge and sufficiently dark sky for this facility. Forest supervisor Stan Stevenson (left) receives a demonstration from SDSC faculty.

FLOOD DAMAGE, TRABUCO TRACT, 1969. In 1965, the Public Land Law Review Commission recommended ending private leases on federal land. The result was the Forest Services' formal ending of the Summer Home Program in 1966. From a high of 349 cabins in 1960, the restriction on new permits and events such as these 1969 floods dropped the Cleveland's total to 318 by 1974.

SMOKEY BEAR GREETING CHILDREN, C. 1963. Forest Service public outreach and education has benefited from America's beloved "Smokey Bear." Created for a World War II fire prevention program in 1944, Smokey Bear was quickly adapted to posters, magazine and newspaper advertisements, comic strips, and public service announcements. In 1950, a rescued bear cub from New Mexico became the living Smokey, housed at the National Zoo in Washington, D.C.

SMOKEY FIRE PREVENTION ADVERTISEMENT, C. 1960. Smokey's 1947 message that "Only YOU Can Prevent Forest Fires" was so successful that in 1952 Congress passed the Smokey Bear Act to protect Smokey's intellectual property. His image and message can be found on toys, films, videos, comic books, pins, brochures, bumper stickers, and calendars—and by 1960 on this bench at Horton Plaza in San Diego.

RANGER PROVIDING EDUCATIONAL PROGRAM, C. 1960. Here a ranger provides a lecture on firefighting to a group of Girl Scouts on a field trip at the Escondido Station. Public outreach included open houses, demonstrations, and guided tours of fire stations, administrative centers, and recreational facilities. Such programs also served as recruiting for future employees.

SUPERVISOR STEVENSON AT LOS PINOS DEDICATION, 1968. The 1960s changed American society. One such program, the Job Corps, brought underprivileged young men to the forest for education, skills training, and job experience. The Cleveland provided the former CCC campsite near El Cariso in exchange for forestry work. For the Cleveland, this program signaled some coming changes for the forest as it moved into a new era.

Five

Environmental Planning for the Next Century 1970–2007

Postwar Americans awakened to a new understanding of the negative effects of unbridled development and consumption of natural resources and open space. The era's massive suburbanization and urban redevelopment changed the focus and tenor of conservation from managed use to protection. Displacement of neighborhoods from federal interstate freeway projects, disclosure of unregulated dumping of toxics, proliferating air and water pollution, and rapid loss of open space and wildlands fueled the newly recoined environmental movement. In response, Congress passed a series of new laws such as the National Environmental Policy Act (NEPA) of 1969 that required all federal projects to be analyzed for their potential adverse effects to the environment and include public participation in the planning and review of such projects. Environmentalists adopted the new interdisciplinary science of ecology, which emphasized the importance of protecting all interrelated components of the environment in order to maintain ecosystems threatened by human overuse and degradation. In 1973, the Endangered Species Act was a direct response, with its regulatory protection of rare, threatened, and endangered plant and animal species. The advent of these, and other, environmental laws protecting natural and cultural resources in the 1960s and 1970s added new challenges for forest staff in managing and administering the Cleveland's lands. This required expanding the forest staff with new resource and planning specialists for addressing these legal and professional mandates. In addition, societal changes brought about from the civil, and women's, rights movements would alter both the perspectives and diversity of the forest staff's makeup. Although federal funding was available for institutional expansion in the 1970s, the Forest Service faced budget cuts leading to staff reductions and major reorganization as it moved into the 1990s. Since that time, the Forest Service has ridden a roller coaster of budgetary cuts and restructuring amid increasing public scrutiny and expectations. For the Cleveland in the last decade, the interrelation of the region's sprawling urbanization with the forest's inherent natural systems, most notably wildfire, has resulted in a renewed public focus on the Cleveland's plans, policies, and practices as it heads into its second century.

SUPERVISORS SMITH, CLARK, AND STEVENSON, C. 1970S. In 1969, the Supervisor's Office was moved from its previous location at Twelfth Avenue and Broadway in downtown San Diego to this uptown building at 3211 Fifth Avenue. Recently retired, Supervisor Stan Stevenson (right) poses with his successor, Ken Clark (center), and Clark's successor, Don Smith (left). In 1991, the Supervisor's Office was moved to a location more central to the forest in Rancho Bernardo.

PUBLIC MEETING, C. 1970S. Public participation is an important aspect of NEPA. These meetings allow forest stakeholders and users to provide input on Cleveland projects. The provisions of NEPA also allow for legal challenges to projects. Although lawsuits have been filed against Cleveland projects, environmental lawsuits such as one challenging a private resort development on Mount Laguna resulted in project cancellation and eventual forest acquisition of the property.

SMOKEY BEAR WITH WOODSY OWL, 1984. In 1971, the Forest Service introduced Woodsy Owl and his tag line, "Give a Hoot, Don't Pollute." In 1997, Woodsy's anti-pollution message received updating for the goals of ecosystem management to "Give a Hand, Care for the Land." Both generously appear at special events such as parades, fairs, schools, air shows, and sporting events at the Cleveland staffs' request.

EARTH DAY EVENT, 1980. Forest public affairs officers (PAO) took a more active role as public participation during the environmental era demanded. PAOs coordinate the Cleveland's annual exhibits at San Diego County's Del Mar Fair, fund-raisers such as the annual Burn Run, and visits from dignitaries such as USFS chiefs and international foresters, and respond to media requests in the new age of instantaneous, real-time news.

FOREST PLANNING PUBLIC MEETING, 1979. The National Forest Management Act of 1974 mandated long-range planning for all national forests. The Cleveland responded with a comprehensive program of specialist study, data analysis, and public participation that resulted in 1986's Land and Resources Management Plan. In 2005, staff updated the plan and in 2007 presented to the public an Adaptive Management Framework process to guide environmental compliance during project implementation.

AGUA TIBIA WILDERNESS TRAILHEAD, 1999. Passage of the Wilderness Act of 1964 provided formalization of the Cleveland's wilderness management areas. In 1974, the forest established boundaries for the 15,394-acre Agua Tibia Wilderness. In 1984, the California Wilderness Act established the 39,540-acre San Mateo Wilderness on the Trabuco District as well as the 13,100-acre Pine Creek and 8,000-acre Hauser Wilderness areas on the Descanso District.

BIOLOGISTS UNDERTAKING PLANT SURVEY, 1984. New planning and environmental compliance mandates such as the Endangered Species Act of 1973 necessitated hiring technical specialists. Resources staff added specialist botanists and wildlife biologists to the core resource team of foresters, geologists, and hydrologists. Permit coordination with regulatory agencies reinforced the essential role natural resource staff play in forest operations.

ARCHAEOLOGIST INSPECTING SITE VANDALISM, C. 1980S. Environmental mandates also included cultural resources. The National Historic Preservation Act of 1966, the Archaeological Resource Protection Act of 1979, and the Native American Graves and Repatriation Act of 1990 all protect historic, archeological, and culturally significant resources. As such, the Cleveland hired its first cultural specialists in the 1980s and established a Heritage Resources Program for stewarding these nonrenewable cultural resources.

PASSPORT IN TIME VOLUNTEERS, 1996. In the 1990s, as the Forest Service celebrated the centennial of the Forest Reserve Act, they helped fund some cultural resource management programs such as the volunteer-based Passport in Time. Forest staff, such as archaeologist and Heritage Program manager Cari VerPlanck (second from top left), helped train and educate volunteers in the management practices and stewardship of significant forest cultural resources.

RECREATION OFFICER BEDFORD CASH WITH VOLUNTEERS, 1987. The Cleveland staff broadened its professional, demographic, and ethnic makeup during this period. Federal laws requiring equal opportunities in hiring were coupled with legislation such as the Volunteers in the Forest Act of 1972 and programs such as the Senior Community Service Employment Program to provide opportunities for all those with talent, time, and energy to assist in forest operations.

FOREST SUPERVISOR ANNE FEGE, 1996. New specialties and technological skills provided opportunities to compete for positions and jobs previously unavailable to women and minority employees. An example of the changing order occurred in 1990 when Dr. Anne S. Fege, Ph.D., was hired as forest supervisor. Another fundamental change shown here is the Data General computer system that linked all USFS locations and employees electronically—before Internet was the Internet!

LAGUNA YACC CREW, 1980. Following the success of the Job Corps program of the late 1960s, the Youth Conservation Corps (YCC) program was established to provide opportunities for male and female youth ages 15 to 19 to spend the summer working on conservation projects. From 1977 to 1981, the Young Adult Conservation Corps (YACC) program provided young adults (ages 16 to 23) work on similar natural resource enhancement projects.

SIERRA PEAK COMMUNICATIONS SITE, 1995. The growing telecommunications industry continued to be major users of forest peaks for their infrastructure needs. Lands and special use officers now had to deal with a myriad of requests for access to key forest locations for media, public safety, phone, satellite, and Internet transmission equipment.

YOUNG BACKPACKERS, 1976. The environmental movement inspired new outdoor recreation. Recreational equipment designed for wilderness exploration, such as backpacks, or activities such as mountain biking, hang gliding, off-roading, and geo-caching challenged forest managers. In the 1990s, the America's Great Outdoors and National Forest Scenic Byways programs were initiated to promote forest recreation opportunities as well as mandates for providing universal access improvements to forest facilities and programs.

CAMPFIRE INTERPRETIVE PROGRAM, 1979. Demand for "traditional" outdoor educational and interpretive programs expanded. Slideshows, guided tours, visitor center and wayside exhibits, interpretive panels, and living history demonstration programs all were part of the Cleveland's interpretive programs. Volunteers were key to interpretive and information programs, helping supplement staff in lean budget times.

LAW ENFORCEMENT OFFICERS, C. 1990S. With hundreds of thousands of visitors annually, public safety and law enforcement became a necessity. Early law enforcement focused on illegal grazing, arson, and vandalism. In the 1970s and 1980s, illegal marijuana plantations and, in the late 1990s, the increase in illegal immigrant traffic through Cleveland required attention from both resource and public safety perspectives. The forest now has fully-trained and certified peace officers providing essential public safety services.

Ecology Conference, 1993. Chief Dale Robertson introduced ecosystem management principles in 1992. Ecosystem management looks to integrate physical, biological, and social/cultural influences into a holistic approach to management decisions and implementation. The Cleveland continues to work with other Southern California national forests, land management agencies, and the public in planning for specific issues such as habitat and species conservation in a regionally viable context.

Brush Fire Flare Up, c. 2000. Although environmental regulation and resource programs gained greatly in this era, fire management still attracts significant attention, resources, and public concern. Technological and training improvements continue, but the dangers of fighting wildland fire is still evident in the tragedies of the crash of two aircraft at Ramona Air Base in 1995 and the loss of firefighters in 1999 (Palomar Mountain) and 2003 (Julian).

PECHANGA FIRE THREATENING TEMECULA, 2000. The 170,000-acre Laguna fire of 1970 was the first significant conflagration to open the question of wildland fire's threats to the developed suburban areas of Southern California. Blamed on the Santa Ana "Devil Winds," the Laguna fire burned significant undeveloped acreage that decades later housed thousands of residents.

CEDAR FIRE DAMAGE, 2003. In October 2003, the incendiary Cedar fire, driven by strong Santa Ana winds, followed brush-fuel deep into suburban San Diego. In the end, the 280,278-acre fire destroyed 2,232 residences and killed 13 civilians and a firefighter. In October 2007, another series of firestorms in San Diego, Orange, and Riverside Counties burned nearly 400,000 acres and destroyed over 1,500 homes while killing seven.

MONTE VISTA COMMUNICATIONS CENTER, 1999. The significant damage to urban areas from the Cedar and 2007 fires challenged the preparedness of regional firefighting agencies. The Cleveland has worked extensively in the last few decades to coordinate with the California Department of Forestry (now CalFire) and other agencies on fire control and suppression. This high-tech communications center provides essential agency coordination during events.

BI-NATIONAL FORESTRY EVENT, 2005. The Cleveland's coordination also includes neighboring Mexico. Former supervisors Ralph Cisco and Mike Rogers initiated efforts to develop and coordinate with Mexican fire agencies in the 1980s. In 2005, the multidisciplinary Border Agency Fire Council (BAFC) celebrated its 10th anniversary. Supervisor Tina Terrell helps Smokey and MAPY (Mexico's forestry mascot) promote the international efforts for forest health, public safety, and fire prevention.

CLEVELAND FIRE CREWS, 1990S AND 1930S. The philosophy, practice, and approach of forest staff over the last 100 years represent many changes. For early watershed advocates such as Abbot Kinney, the fact that the region receives nearly all of its water from nonlocal sources would be significantly different, but the continued focus on fire management for protection of the private property of the region's residents would be recognizable. Forest Service founder Gifford Pinchot would likely be surprised at the refocus of his "resources for use" brand of conservation to the focus on the myriad environmental mandates for resource preservation. What previous Cleveland managers would certainly not be surprised with would be that, although the faces of the Cleveland National Forest have changed, the dedication, sacrifice, hard work—and can-do attitude—of its staff have not.

A Toast for the Cleveland, Thanks! This book is dedicated to all the rangers, firefighters, managers, administrators, support staff, resource specialists, design professionals, interpreters, maintenance workers, contractors, volunteers, constituents, critics, one-time visitors, and regular users who have made the efforts to care. For those who spent, and sometimes gave, their lives for the Cleveland National Forest, the underlying public interest, and your fellow citizens' private property, your sacrifices are rewarded with every visitor spiritually rejuvenated by the opportunity to separate themselves, if just for a moment, from the urban world and by everyone who connects with the natural world and cultural heritage inherent in this public reserve. Cheers!

BIBLIOGRAPHY

Cermak, Robert W. *Fire in the Forest: A History of Forest Fire Control on the National Forests in California, 1898–1956*. California: USDA Forest Service Pacific Southwest Region, 2005.

Cleveland National Forest Historical Archives. Manuscripts, photographs, technical reports, maps, primary and secondary source materials. Palomar District Office, Ramona, CA.

Godfrey, Anthony. *The Ever-Changing View: A History of the National Forests in California*. California: USDA Forest Service Pacific Southwest Region, 2005.

Huber, James Anthony. *Abbot Kinney: Champion of California's Forests and Watersheds*. San Diego, CA: M.A. thesis, San Diego State University, 1992.

Lockmann, Ronald F. *Guarding the Forests of Southern California: Evolving Attitudes Toward Conservation of Watershed, Woodlands, and Wilderness*. Glendale, CA: The Arthur H. Clark Company, 1981.

Miller, Char, ed. *American Forests: Nature, Culture, and Politics*. Lawrence, KS: University of Kansas Press, 1997.

Newland, James D. *Historic Resources Survey & Evaluation Report: Administrative Structures*. San Diego, CA: USDA Forest Service Cleveland National Forest, 1995.

———. *Historic Resources Survey & Evaluation Report: Recreation Residences and Special Use Resorts—Descanso District*. San Diego, CA: USDA Forest Service Cleveland National Forest, 1995.

Palmer, Christine Savage. *Civilian Conservation Corps Structures on the Cleveland National Forest, California, 1933–1942*. San Diego, CA: USDA Forest Service Cleveland National Forest, 1993.

Robinson, John W. and Bruce D. Risher. *The San Jacintos: The Mountain Country from Banning to Borrego Valley*. Arcadia, CA: Big Santa Anita Historical Society, 1993.

Sakarias, Michael. *Cleveland National Forest: San Diego's Watershed*. San Diego, CA: senior thesis, San Diego State University, 1974.

Steen, Harold K., ed. *The Origins of the National Forests: A Centennial Symposium*. Durham, NC: Forest History Society, 1992.

Supernowicz, Dana. *Historical Evaluation of the Trabuco, Holy Jim, San Juan, and Hot Springs Summer Home Tracts on the Trabuco Ranger District, Cleveland National Forest*. San Diego, CA: USDA Forest Service Cleveland National Forest, 1994.

West, Terry L. *Centennial Mini-Histories of the Forest Service*. Washington, D.C.: USDA Forest Service, 1992.

Williams, Gerald W. *The USDA Forest Service—The First Century*. Washington, D.C.: USDA Forest Service, 2000.

Across America, People are Discovering Something Wonderful. *Their Heritage.*